SAINTS, SINNERS & SHORTSTOPS

SAINTS, SINNERS & SHORTSTOPS

4 Wars • 40 Countries • 4,000 Characters

Jim Becker

FOREIGN CORRESPONDENT

The Celadon Press

For rights information or to submit requests, please contact:
Jellinek & Murray Literary Agency
2024 Mauna Place
Honolulu, HI 96822
TEL: 808 521 4057
Fax: 808 521 4058
r.jellinek@verizon.net

Editor: Roger Jellinek
Design by Bill Greaves, Concept West
Jacket design by Bill Greaves
Author photograph by Nathalie Walker
Copy editor: Sandie Osborne
Production editor: Michele DeFilippo, 1106 Design

Printed in China.

Cartoon by Corky, Copyright ©2006 by Corky Trinidad.

"THE DAY THE GOVS WON IT ALL"
Reprinted by permission from *Honolulu Star-Bulletin*.

Distributed by Bess Press, Inc.
3565 Harding Avenue
Honolulu, Hawaii 96816
Tel: (808) 734-7159

Becker, Jim.
    Saints, sinners & shortstops : 4 wars, 40 countries, 4,000 characters
    / Jim Becker. -- 1st ed. -- Honolulu, HI : Celadon Press, 2006.
        p. ; cm.
        ISBN-13: 978-159975-834-3
        ISBN-10: 1-59975-834-2
        1. Becker, Jim. 2. Foreign correspondents--United States--
    Biography. 3. Sportswriters--United States--Biography. 4. Critics--
    United States--Biography. 5. Journalists--United States--Biography.
    6. Athletes--United States--Anecdotes. 7. Celebrities--United
    States--Anecdotes. 8. Politicians--United States--Anecdotes.
    9. United States--History--20th century--Anecdotes. I. Title.
II. Saints, sinners and shortstops.

PN4874.B434 A3 2006

    070.4/332/092--dc22   0604

To Bob and Ida Rhea, for their friendship

All the world's a stage,
And all the men and women merely players.
They have their exits and their entrances
And each man in his time plays many parts . . .

—William Shakespeare, *As You Like It*

CONTENTS

Part Four—We Had Chop Suey

FOREWORD

If careers are checkered, Jim Becker's is a chessboard. From Hawaii to Brooklyn, Bayreuth, Babylon and Botswana (Hawaii's Antipode) this multi-faceted newsman has crisscrossed every square on the board, collecting along the way fascinating stories about heroes, saints, sinners and celebrities.

He tells these stories in this delightful book, stories about such diverse characters as General George C. Marshall and Marilyn Monroe, Joe DiMaggio, Margaret Thatcher, Jackie Robinson, Lyndon Baines Johnson, Jack Nicklaus, the "right Dalai Lama" and scores more.

For a decade Jim Becker and I faced each other every day as fellow columnists on either side of the editorial page of the Honolulu Star-Bulletin. We were mutually admiring bookends. Besides the column, Jim reveled in his sideline as drama and music critic, and even chipped in a weekly sports column. Those stories are in the book, too, Bette Midler and Mayor Frank Fasi and a bunch of high school kids from the tough part of town who had their greatest day.

Impossibly precocious, my fellow bookend relates how his career and his lifelong passion for the arts, the latter still evident in his broadcasts and standing-room-only opera lectures, were born in his teens, when he collected tales of Charlie Chaplin and Bugsy Siegel, Sergei Rachmaninoff and the majestic Marian Anderson.

In Jim Becker's lifetime of legends—whether they are stories, historic events or the people who prompt them—he has become one himself.

"Jim you've got to write a book," urged his legion of fans and friends. Happily, he has. I just wish it were twice as long.

Read all about it.

—Cobey Black
Columnist and author
Honolulu, 2005

PREFACE

"It must be great to be 17," said the City Editor of the *Los Angeles Herald-Express* as he checked a story I had just submitted, "but there is only one R in erection." In the exuberance of youth I had doubled the R's in the word.

And I knew right then that this news business was going to be fun.

The City Editor was Jack Berger. I had finagled a job as a reporter with him shortly after my 17th birthday. Jack Berger taught me not only how to spell, but how to write a news story and how to meet a deadline (we had seven a day on the *Herald*). And he turned me loose to report on many of the characters they make movies about these days, from Charlie Chaplin and Errol Flynn to Bugsy Siegel and Seabiscuit.

He launched me on a journey that eventually included four wars, assorted revolutions, riots, assassinations, royal weddings and a day with a bunch of Hawaiian, Samoan, Filipino and Japanese high school kids in Honolulu that produced the most important story I ever wrote.

The trip included brushes with presidents (one of whom, LBJ, called me a "no good stupid lying son of a bitch" when I told him the truth about the war in Vietnam) and prime ministers (the most remarkable of which was Margaret Thatcher), athletes and artists, kooks and clowns and even the occasional statesman.

It was a glorious life; I would have paid my bosses for the privilege. Lucky for me, they thought of paying me first.

The thread that connected all these adventures, for a half century and more, was Hawaii, the place and its people, so fortuitously located between East and West, a figurative and physical bridge.

My roots in Hawaii run deep. The Army gave me a brief look on my way home from World War II service, and although I spent much of it wrangling with a customs officer, I had time enough to begin the lifelong love affair. Five years later the AP sent me to Honolulu as a correspondent. Five years after that back as Chief of the Hawaii Bureau. I reported about the great labor disputes which disrupted and then destroyed the ruling oligarchy, sugar, pineapple, shipping and the larger-than-life figures on both sides: The Australian Harry Bridges, accused of Communist Party affiliations and his burly, brainy Hawaii deputy, Jack Hall and on the management side the self-assured fifth and sixth generation sons and daughters of the missionaries who came to Hawaii in the early 19th century to do good and famously stayed to do well.

I watched the transfer of power from those who owned the great plantations to the sons and daughters of the immigrants who came from Asia to work them. I was even assigned as an official witness to the last scheduled execution in Hawaii, luckily cancelled with five minutes to spare.

I sat in the Legislature meeting room in Iolani Palace, the one-time home of the Hawaiian monarchs, on a lazy summer afternoon and heard the Territorial governor tell visiting senators that in Hawaii everybody is in the minority, true then, true now, one of the major charms of the place.

Always, no matter where my travels took me, I came home. For nearly a decade I wrote a human interest column for the *Honolulu Star-Bulletin*. I established the connection with Hawaii's antipode, Botswana, which led to dozens of young women from the southern African country attending university when none had before. I discovered Bette Midler, or rather she discovered me. And I detailed in a front page story the day a bunch of kids collected from Hawaii's racial rainbow won the City high school championship and changed lives in their community, a story that reverberates today and is the climax of this collection.

The world come to us: Nixon (pre-Watergate), Bill Clinton (post-Monica), the union leader Jimmy Hoffa (pre-disappearance), one of my toughest-talking interviews ever, but I respected him and he me and many more you will meet in these pages.

Preface

I wrote and lectured on theater, opera, ballet, symphony, even Elvis Presley, who made one of his first public appearances in Hawaii. He had a toothache and my dentist, who fixed it, told me Elvis' steady diet of Cokes and French fries had resulted in the worst set of teeth he had ever encountered.

I probed the history of the Islands, and that of the December 7 attack on Pearl Harbor, both the bombers and the bombed.

In the pages that follow are my stories about some of the people and places that made the serious work of reporting the news so much fun. You'll meet Jackie Robinson (I covered his first major league game, an event of transcendental importance to our nation), the Dalai Lama, (during the transcendental tragedy occurring in his nation). And you'll encounter Baron X, Bette Midler and the Beatles, Rachmaninoff and Pete Rose (he lied to me, too).

You'll visit Bayreuth and Botswana and the Taj Mahal. You'll witness the Cuban Missile Crisis (I was on the plane that photographed the Soviet freighters taking the missiles out of Cuba) and the Munich Olympics massacre of Israeli team members, where international terrorism first reared its ugly head.

You'll join me in my interview with Senator Joseph McCarthy (of the 'ism' that bears his name) before he discovered Communism, hence the subject never came up. And you'll dine with me and Imelda Marcos in Manila before she and her husband stole their country blind, so that subject never came up either. And you'll meet Princess Diana before she married her prince (she taught pre-school across the street from our London apartment house; I also covered the royal wedding) and Marilyn Monroe before she made her famous tour of Korea to entertain the troops. I helped arrange it.

And the man who led the Japanese raid on Pearl Harbor as well as the American intelligence officers on the ground that December day, telling what each knew and when they knew it.

Some of the stories are amusing, some touching, some life-affirming. All are of a time when reporters shared the belief that a profession important enough to be protected by the very First Amendment to the Constitution had a resultant responsibility to readers and viewers to shed light on issues and events, rather than to play non-stop "Gotcha."

Shining that light was at least half the fun.

PART ONE–
URGENT BECKER

1.
THE RIGHT DALAI LAMA

At least two movies have been made about his life and he has appeared on almost every TV talk show on three continents over the years, but there was a time when the 14th Dalai Lama, the Tibetan "god-king," was the most mysterious human being on earth. Photographs of the Dalai Lama were as rare as interviews with Greta Garbo or World Series victories for the Chicago Cubs.

It was once claimed that only seven westerners had ever set eyes on the Dalai Lama in his secluded Himalayan Kingdom. One of them, Heinrich Harrer, a German who spent seven years as an advisor to the Dalai Lama and wrote a book about it, has had his life made into a movie, too.

So when in March 1959 the Dalai Lama decided to flee, on foot, to India ahead of the Chinese takeover of his country, it was the major international news story of the day. The usual suspects among the foreign corresponding corps, of which I was one, were dispatched to India to report on and, most importantly, to photograph his flight to freedom.

The Indian authorities, including Prime Minister Nehru who had grudgingly granted asylum to the Dalai Lama—the Chinese were touchy on the subject—arranged for the exile and his entourage to enter India at a town called Tezpur, which had an airstrip and the communications with the outside world needed to carry the report to the headquarters of all news organizations.

Photographs, however, were another matter. Given the primitive communications of the day (no cell or video phones; even satellites were not in general use), the only method of dispatching photographs was via a single "Radiophoto" circuit from Calcutta, several hundred miles southeast of Tezpur, to London.

The Radiophoto circuit could send but one picture at a time, and each took nearly 20 minutes to transmit.

The circuit was the target of the two major news agencies in the field. The one who managed to convey a photograph from Tezpur to the Radiophoto office in Calcutta and file it first would score a considerable journalistic scoop, a word then still in vogue.

I did everything I could think of to ensure that AP would file that first picture. I chartered an airplane to fly the film from Tezpur to Calcutta. (So did UPI.) I arranged for a fast car with a manic driver to speed the precious cargo from the airport to the Radiophoto office in town on a dusty, two-lane road crammed constantly with sacred cows, jaywalking villagers unaware of the threat posed by a speeding motorcar, pedicabs, pushcarts and countless pye-dogs who moved reluctantly from their resting places in the middle of the road. I engaged a crew of Indian boys with AP signs to form a human chain that would direct us from the airplane to the waiting car. And I bought the only photographic shop with a darkroom in the vicinity of the Radiophoto office. (One of the best deals AP ever made; after the event I sold it at a slight profit.)

Then there was nothing to do but wait. It was a dangerous time in South Asia. India and Pakistan were growing increasingly antagonistic, a feeling that would build into a major shooting war in a few years. The

Chinese were exceedingly anxious about intrusions into their air space, which they declared now included Tibet. This precluded any attempt to fly into it to check on the Dalai Lama's progress.

Nehru was nervous, too. He hated the spotlight beaming on his impending guest at a time when he was trying to placate his Chinese neighbors. Border skirmishes and discrepancies between Indian and Chinese maps had resulted in a sometimes acrimonious exchange with China in the 1950s called Hindi-Chini bhai-bhai (Hindi for "India and China are brother"). Nehru got a shooting war with China in 1962 for his pains.

In the midst of these powder kegs, the gaggle of foreign correspondents gathered at the Great Eastern Hotel in Calcutta, eyeing each other warily and waiting for the signal to fly to Tezpur and meet the mysterious refugee.

During this vigil, a correspondent for the *Daily Express* of London, then a newspaper with pretensions of importance, decided to give us a lesson in British tabloid journalism. The correspondent excused himself from a gathering in the hotel bar—just as his turn to buy a round approached—and was gone for half an hour or so. Not long after his return, many of us received angry cables from our home offices demanding that we match an exclusive Daily Express story describing in copious detail the Dalai Lama's entourage as it made its way through the foothills of Tibet to impending freedom in India.

The *Express* correspondent had, of course, repaired to his hotel room and concocted the story out of whole cloth. It began with the fetching lead, "I flew over the Dalai Lama today," went on to name the plane's pilot (a fictitious tea planter), and described in flamboyant detail the spinning prayer wheels and fluttering banners of the procession.

Juicy stuff, to be sure, and invented within the walls of his own hotel room. I'd been in the business for 15 years by then and I was outraged at this exercise in journalistic fiction. Several of my colleagues, on the other hand, like the characters in Evelyn Waugh's great newspaper novel *Scoop*, were angry only that they hadn't thought of the ruse first.

Soon after, word came that the Dalai Lama and his party were indeed approaching the Indian border, and we all flew to Tezpur to cover the real story, and to take those precious photographs and rush them back to the Radiophoto office and file them—FIRST!

The refugee procession made it into town. There were no fluttering banners or spinning prayer wheels, just dusty shaven-headed monks in saffron-colored robes, including the Dalai Lama himself, a small and shy man who nevertheless appeared pleased to have reached safety.

The Dalai Lama was led to a platform and a microphone which the Indian government had provided for a news conference. Standing alongside his interpreter, a husky Indian with a beard and a lovely head of wavy hair, he submitted to questions from the press corps. He had no English at this time, and was very cagey in his own language, perhaps because in his wildest nightmares he'd never dreamt of venturing so far from his sheltered palace or subjugating himself to the scrutiny of so many strange-looking individuals.

After the conference we wrote and dispatched our stories, and then the race was on to get the pictures to the office in Calcutta, and thence to London and the waiting world.

The plane carrying AP's precious cargo of film, and the less important occupants such as the photographer and me, sped down the runway and took off almost simultaneously with the UPI plane.

Whereupon my best-laid plans began immediately to unravel. The direct route, and the fastest, from Tezpur to Calcutta was right over India's neighbor, East Pakistan (now Bangladesh). The previous day, the Pakistanis had shot down an Indian Air Force plane that they claimed (probably correctly) was taking pictures of Pakistani military installations, and they announced they would shoot down any other planes intruding in Pakistani airspace.

This warning was not lost upon the pilot of the AP plane. He refused to risk the direct flight, choosing instead to fly around East Pakistan, adding at least half an hour to our flight time. The UPI pilot apparently had no such fears, and fortunately for him, if not for me, was not shot down.

Hence when the photographer and I arrived at the Calcutta airport we were informed that the UPI plane had landed well before us. We did our best to make up the time. We dashed down the chain of AP signs to the waiting car, whose driver blew his horn non-stop all the way to town, scattering cows, roosters and villagers with no distinctions. We rushed into our darkroom, developed three photos—the limit was three—and I hustled next door to the Radiophoto office with three wet prints over my arm. Too late. Three UPI Radiophotos were on file ahead of me, and the first one was just about to be transmitted. I had lost in a photo finish, thanks to a chicken pilot.

This defeat did not escape the attention of the AP photo editors in London. Within minutes I received the first of an increasingly furious series of cables, all marked URGENT, at about two bucks a word. It read:

URGENT BECKER UPI DALAI LAMA PHOTO ROLLING NOW HOW OURS PLEASE. AP PHOTOS LONDON

In journalistic cable-ese, "HOW OURS" is not a polite request for feeble excuses about craven pilots. It is a scream of anguish, a veiled threat that you can be replaced, a demand for action.

I tried bribery, cajolery, even threats of suicide in an attempt to get one of my photos moved up in the queue, to no avail.

Soon came a second cable: URGENT BECKER SECOND UPI DALAI LAMA PHOTO ROLLING NOW OUR SUBSCRIBERS UPSET ANXIOUS. AP PHOTOS LONDON

The third one was even nastier.

I began contemplating another line of work, something less stressful, after I received the following:

URGENT BECKER OUR FIRST DALAI LAMA PHOTO ROLLING NOW FIFTY SEVEN MINUTES AFTER OPPOSITION. AP PHOTOS LONDON

Bad news, indeed. But within minutes the sky cleared and the birds began to sing and all was right with the AP world. I was handed a fourth cable:

URGENT BECKER UPI DALAI LAMA FULL HAIRED. OUR DALAI LAMA SHORN CLARIFY URGENTLY. AP PHOTOS LONDON

And I knew right away that God had saddled me with a cowardly pilot but he had more than leveled the playing field by matching me with a UPI correspondent named Earnest Hobrecht, who was almost certainly the only member of the entire foreign press corps who had no idea what the real Dalai Lama must look like.

People who worked with him told me that Ernie was one of those journalistic accidents, a classic example of the Peter Principle in action. He was, I believe, a salesman who was promoted to newsman when a vacancy suddenly appeared and he was available. He probably could not have located Tibet on a map and he was obviously uninformed about the tonsorial habits of Tibetan monks.

Ernie had sent three Radiophotos of the wrong man. He had sent photos of the wavy-haired and bearded Indian interpreter, who was, after all, the man standing behind the microphone. And to make certain that a good clear picture emerged at the other end of the Radio-photo circuit, Ernie had carefully cropped out of each picture the insignificant shorn man in the monk's robe who was standing next to the Indian interpreter—the Dalai Lama.

Two things then happened simultaneously. One man handed me a copy of the *The Statesman,* the excellent newspaper published just down the street, and he passed me another cable from London. I looked at *The Statesman* first. There, on the front page was a huge, six-column blank space. It was where a photo of the Dalai Lama was to have appeared. Then I read the cable:

URGENT BECKER UPI SENT THREE RADIOPHOTOS OF THE WRONG MAN AND WERE FORCED TO KILL THEIR PHOTOS ALL OVER THE WORLD REGARDS AP PHOTOS LONDON

Regards indeed. The first kind words I had heard all day.

All became clear. *The Statesman* had planned to run the photo six columns wide on its front page, and received the KILL order just in time to chisel the photo out of the plate used to print the front page, leaving a huge blank space.

I then wrote the cable that has passed into journalistic legend:

URGENT AP PHOTOS LONDON THE BEST DALAI LAMA IS THE RIGHT DALAI LAMA. REGARDS BECKER

I went back to the hotel, where the news of the killed photos had preceded me. The assembled press corps insisted that I mount the bar and relate, in detail, the tale of the right Dalai Lama.

Ernie was not there to enjoy it. He had retired to his room and did not emerge for two days. The next I heard of him, he was selling real estate in Oklahoma, I believe.

When I finished the story, grown men collapsed around me in tears of joy and spasms of laughter.

When composure was restored, several members of the audience insisted that I tell it again, and I did, and I have ever since, at the gatherings of foreign correspondents, in Tokyo or Washington, New York or London.

2.
GETTING JUMP-STARTED

One of the 20th Century's most celebrated newspapermen—a proud term in its time—was Stanley Walker, the city editor of the best newspaper ever published in our country, the *New York Herald-Tribune*. Stanley Walker surveyed the journalistic scene of his era and cogently declared: "The best newspapermen, like the best prize fighters, come out of the gutter."

He made the observation during the Great Depression, which sent millions of American families into the economic gutter, from which they had to fight their own way out. My family landed there, a house full of kids and a father whose occupation had shriveled to almost nothing. My mother regularly took the entire brood to charity clinics (I can still smell the carbolic acid they used to disinfect them), bought us pairs of used shoes from the Salvation Army and regularly pawned the living room sofa for ready cash. I can remember to this day the howl of anguish she let out when she got only $10 instead of the customary $15 when she pawned it. (Five bucks bought a lot of used shoes.) When my father found work—any job, anywhere, any time—she would ransom the sofa back. You could tell the state of the family finances by whether there was a place to sit down in the living room.

We lived in a poor part of town—South Central Los Angeles—because we were poor. So was almost everybody. One day I came home from school, aged about seven, and discovered my father was on the front steps discussing things with two men who had come to disconnect our telephone for lack of payment. The telephone was vital to my father's existence. A "juicer," or electrician, at the movie studios, he managed to get a day or two of work every month, and these jobs were handed out in strict rotation by telephone.

My father was brandishing a baseball bat. He had been a good semi-pro baseball player, and retained some of the tools of that trade, which he gradually passed on to me. "You can turn off the telephone," my father explained to the two men, "but if you do I will kill you."

This was Papa Bear stuff, and as Baby Bear, I looked into my father's eyes and knew that he meant what he said. The two men came to the same conclusion and they went away, leaving the telephone in working order.

I recount these almost Dickensian childhood experiences merely to establish my qualifications for the Stanley Walker Seal of Approval. In point of fact, my entire childhood is wrapped in a golden glow of memory. I loved it, all of it. We played every sport in season and practically invented midnight basketball. School was a snap. And I seemed to dominate every new classroom or playground life presented to me.

Of course we were not angels. I recall standing in front of the May Company department store in downtown L.A. when one of my football teammates complained, "Shee, man, I stole the wrong size shoes." He went right back in and stole the right size.

Growing up thusly amidst real people, instead of some isolated leafy suburb had an additional advantage. It afforded me the inestimable privilege of attending inner city public schools. In such educational establishments not a great deal of time was wasted on building self-esteem. We were instead drilled constantly on reading and writing.

There also was an emphasis on the real world into which we were due to be flung and expected to earn a living.

At Foshay Junior High, where I was the only white kid on the school baseball team, we were sat down in groups and directed to write about how we would make that living. We were not to indulge in any airy-fairy speculations about working for world peace or saving the whales. We were to describe what kind of job we would seek.

This was no problem for me.

My father took me to my very first football game when I was literally a babe in arms. I could keep a baseball score card by the time I was three.

As a result I was an inveterate newspaper reader, particularly of the sports pages. The hot shot columnists captured my attention, as well. I could imitate each of their styles.

I was also a constant movie viewer. I had a cousin who ushered at the neighborhood theater who let me in the side door and I never missed a movie. It was a time when newspaper movies were the rage. *The Front Page* made a deep impression on me, as well as its many clones, notably *His Girl Friday*. I was stirred by Hitchcock's *Foreign Correspondent* starring Joel McCrae. Foreign correspondents in the movies wore trench coats and dashed from capital to capital on unlimited expense accounts, and as a kid whose only foreign experience had been a family trip to Tijuana, that life had immense appeal to me.

(In time I would have three trench coats in my closet, one for every season, and an AP pass good on every airline and hotel in the world, long before credit cards were invented.)

So writing down my ambitions was a real no-brainer. I wrote that I wanted to be a sportswriter, and a foreign correspondent, and a columnist. I added that I hoped to make $100 a week, an immense sum at the time. (The football coach Vince Lombardi once told me he was glad to land a job during the Great Depression coaching all sports and teaching physics and mathematics at a high school in New Jersey for $150 a month. For nine months.)

My literary effort was published—my first byline—in the *Foshay Facts,* the school newspaper. The die having been cast, when I graduated from high school at the age of 16, in the midst of World War II, I headed straight to the *Los Angeles Times* (in those days a newspaper produced by grown-ups) because it was closest to home. I was promptly hired as a copy boy for $14 a week. The tasks of a copy boy consisted of fetching coffee for the reporters and rewrite men and sitting on a long bench waiting for a writer to finish a story, at which time he would shout "copy" and the copy boy on the end would rush over, collect it and deliver it to the city desk, then the hub of all newspaper operations.

Due to the war, most of my fellow copy boys were girls, including the head copy boy, so in addition to growing up color blind in inner city schools I quickly acquired gender blindness too.

I was a big kid, extremely noticeable and street smart. I quickly discovered which reporters liked their coffee laced with bourbon. (There was a bottle of it in the filing cabinet under B; scotch was filed under W.)

It was a hard-drinking racket then, and remained so until the early '60s, when it somehow ceased to be fun, and most of us, including us renowned booze fighters, gave it up.

In a few weeks, one of the assistant city editors decided it was time for me to make the next move up the journalistic ladder, and arranged a job for me with an outfit called City News Service, which distributed news stories (mostly rewritten from the big dailies, of which there were four in Los Angeles) to the smaller suburban newspapers, and also supplied pool reporters to cover the police and emergency services beats during the midnight hours. Each of the four dailies kept a reporter on those beats all day. At night a reporter from City News Service would take over, collect the details of any potential stories, and turn them over to the regular beat reporters when they came to work at dawn.

My boss was the wife of the proprietor of City News who had gone off to war. She taught me many things about the news business, but not the least of which was her instructions on how to tie a Windsor knot, which she demonstrated in ticker tape. To this day it is the only necktie knot I can tie.

After a brief, but useful spell at rewriting news stories I graduated to the late night police beat. At the time I was seriously enamored of a young lady named Zelda DuBois, the granddaughter of W.E.B. DuBois, one of the founders of the NAACP. Zelda knew everybody in the black community and almost everybody else in Hollywood. Through Zelda I played golf with the Mills Brothers, smoked pot in the basement of a theater on Central Avenue with members of Benny Carter's band, and drank whiskey out of coffee cups with Billie Holiday, known as Lady Day, or just Lady to her friends. At least Zelda and I drank whiskey out of coffee cups, Lady drank coffee. It was a time when she was on the wagon.

The coffee cups were because of a wartime ruling that bars could not sell booze after midnight. Some considered this a hardship but the New York restaurateur Toots Shor, popular with players and sportswriters, brushed it off. "If you ain't drunk by midnight you ain't trying," he sagely observed.

So when the magical hour struck, the waiters in the little joint where Lady was singing would whisk away the glasses of whiskey and substitute them with coffee cups full of the forbidden stuff.

Zelda also was a fervent Communist, as was her entire family, and she hauled me to all the Party functions in town, at which I got the full dose of the whole class warfare routine. I quickly decided that this stuff wouldn't influence an alert 11-year-old but I never told Zelda. Charlie Chaplin was a regular speaker at these affairs, and the young Ronald Reagan, bucking for the job he later landed as president of the Screen Actors Guild, dropped in from time to time to nurse his constituency.

Zelda was the agent of my big break, one that jump-started my career. One evening when I was manning the telephones at the police press room Zelda went to a big party at the Sunset Towers apartment of the gangster Bugsy Siegel, at that time the mob's bag man in Hollywood.

The Sunset Towers apartments straddled the city-county line and was full of well-known people, some savory, some not, which caused both the city and county law enforcement agencies to leave the investigation of any wrong doings to the other, which generally meant they went unreported by either.

Among the numerous guests at the party was a hunk named Jon Hall, who specialized in Tarzan-type pictures. He had been married to a singer named Frances Langford, who at the time was touring with Bob Hope entertaining the troops.

Sometime after midnight a misunderstanding arose. One of Siegel's henchmen apparently misconstrued a friendly conversation Hall was having with Virginia Hill, Bugsy's girl, as an advance. The said minion pulled a knife and cut a gash in Hall's nose. This put an immediate damper on proceedings, and the guests began to scatter.

Bleeding profusely, Hall was bundled out of the apartment into a cab and taken to a private hospital for repairs. He left a trail of blood all over the front steps.

No one, of course, called the police of either jurisdiction. But Zelda called me and told me everything she knew.

I took it from there. I talked on the phone to the building superintendent, who had seen Hall hustled into a taxicab. He gave me the taxi's number, and also told me all about the blood on the front steps.

I found the cab driver, and through him the name of the private hospital, and there was a nurse who described the activities there.

(It has never ceased to amaze me what people will tell a reporter. In those days they talked to the press the way people do these days to television cameras.)

Zelda gave me names of other guests, and I got their descriptions of the scene.

And when I had all my facts in place, and a source for every one, I looked around the press room, and I thought, the four guys who work for the four major papers will be coming to work soon, and I am expected to give them all this information and let them run with it.

And I thought, further, 15 or 20 years from now, these same four guys will be doing these same jobs. But I won't.

And I decided to double-cross them.

I sneaked down the hall and found a telephone and called the *Herald-Express*, the biggest newspaper in town and the one that would most appreciate a story with blood and tears and gangsters and Hollywood names.

I asked for Jack Berger, who I had never met. "Mr. Berger, I have your front page story," I told him when he came on the line. He listened, then turned me over to one of the three word wizards who manned the rewrite battery on the *Herald*. I unloaded the story, names, places, quotes, the lot. When I finished, Berger came back on the line. "Nice job, kid," he said.

"You know Mr. Berger," I pointed out, "I am now unemployed."

"What do you make?" he asked. I told a little lie. "I'll double it," Berger said. "You now work for me."

I didn't even go back to the press room to collect the raincoat I had left on the rack. Berger sent somebody else to fetch it.

And some 15 years later, after two wars and assorted other attention-getting assignments, I was in L.A. as part of a speaker tour for the AP, and I mustered the courage to visit the police press room. Three of the four reporters I had double-crossed were there, still doing the same job. When I entered the room, they stood up and applauded.

3.
METHODICAL MADNESS

The *Los Angeles Herald-Express,* known affectionately in its ranks as "the paper for people who move their mouths when they read," was like most newspapers across the country in the days when print was king, a madhouse. But there was a method to it.

The city room was bursting with talent, although short on journalism degrees. Looking back, I don't think we had any. At least two dozen books, ranging from history to humor, came from its writers, and many of us were frequently published over the years in anthologies.

My only objection to the place—although I was a staunch Newspaper Guild member—was that union rules decreed a five-day, 40-hour week. As it was, Jack Berger often had to chase me out at the end of the working day. Otherwise I might have spent nights on the couch in the library, which was often enough occupied by a fellow reporter who had been overcome by strong drink. Work began at 5 a.m. on the *Herald* and continued at a furious pace, with a brief respite at 8 a.m., the time when bars opened legally under wartime restrictions. Then a hefty number of staff members would repair to the Press Café across the street for a morning pick-me-up.

Jack Berger ruled over all. He took me in hand, taught me to spell and to write a tight news story, a talent I retained for many years until it was spoiled by the freedoms afforded a columnist. Berger discouraged any such purple flights. Early one day he called me over and tossed a literary effort back at me.

"I don't understand that thing," he said, "and if I can't understand it, what chance has someone who is stupid enough to buy our newspaper?" Point taken.

In a few weeks I was initiated into the fine art of what was known in the trade as "Picture Stealing." In those pre-TV days, newspapers were in fierce competition to be first to print photos of the victims—preferably young and female—of foul crimes and misdemeanors. The *Herald* had tipsters everywhere, many in the ranks of law enforcement, who supplied names and addresses of foul play. A reporter was immediately dispatched to the home with the hope of arriving before any other reporters and the police. The object was to talk the grieving relatives into temporarily parting with every photograph in the house, and to hustle them back to the office for splash treatment—a full page if possible—in the next edition.

This was tricky work because its exponents were forced to offer condolences, sometimes even to break the bad news, and switch swiftly to the appeal for the photographs and depart the premises in five minutes or less. Many of us may have had success at this intricate endeavor because we came from the Stanley Walker school. We were working class and never lost that people touch.

Problems did arise from time to time when an over-zealous picture-stealer discovered no one at home, and decided to let himself into the premises and scout for photos. We had a cooperative relationship with the police, for the most part, but such actions were considered over the line. Now and again a *Herald* reporter would be tossed in the clink for a day or two as a salutary warning. I was never caught.

L.A. had its own Jack the Ripper, a man who mutilated the sexual organs of his victims, all prostitutes. Shortly after 5 a.m., his fourth victim was found, slashed to a bloody mess in the killer's trademark fashion. I was sent to the grisly scene and managed to get the story into the first edition. The culprit had signed his own name to the hotel register, and dozens of witnesses had seen him take the girl to the room, so it was fairly easy to find him. He was, in fact, chatting up what he apparently planned to make his fifth victim when he was arrested, just in time for our Home Edition. And he confessed in time for our Street Final.

Berger dispatched me the next day to find the intended victim who had slipped back into the netherworld. I scoured the depths of the seedy part of town, but eventually I found her, and managed to *borrow*, not steal, every personal picture she owned for the story.

Soon came my big time reporting period. I was assigned, first as a caddie, then as a colleague, to the great Agness Underwood, the best newspaperman on the entire West Coast, and maybe anywhere. Agness was a class member of the Stanley Walker class. Her husband walked out on her in the depths of the Depression, leaving her with two kids and no skills. Aggie had gotten a job in 1926 as a telephone operator at the *Los Angeles Evening Record* and one day the city editor found himself with no reporters on hand and a story to be covered, so he drafted Aggie, and she never looked back. By 1935 she was doing general assignments at the *Herald-Express*, where she would become city editor in 1947, the first woman in such a position.

Aggie was a star. Her instincts were infallible, her methods direct. Every cop, from the chief on down, was terrified of her. When Aggie arrived at the scene of a crime, often with me in tow, the police lines parted like the Red Sea for Moses. She would personally interrogate witnesses, while the cops stood by taking notes. She never wasted a minute or forgot any of our seven deadlines.

"It's 10:28," she would instruct me. "Go get me a phone."

In time I was promoted from finding phones for Aggie to working alongside her. Together we covered the trial of Charlie Chaplin in federal court for violating the 1910 Mann Act which forbade transporting women across state lines for immoral purposes. Chaplin beat that rap because he was innocent. Aggie had sequestered the only public telephone on the courtroom floor, and when the verdict came in I rushed to it to relay the news, but when I picked it up I discovered some wily rival had cut the cord.

I began to sputter complaints about such unsportsmanlike behavior, but Aggie stopped me cold. "Get your ass to another telephone, and be quick about it," she said. And I did.

Later Chaplin lost a paternity suit involving the same woman, this time in Superior Court. Chaplin was innocent of that charge, too, but the jury didn't like him and found him guilty, and I suppose with our justice system, 50-50 isn't bad. He was ordered to pay child support for a child that wasn't his. The evidence was an inadmissible blood test.

Aggie and I had also teamed up for the trial of Errol Flynn for cavorting with under-age tramps (15 and 17). He was guilty but he got away with it largely because the all-female jury didn't like the two girls and felt they were "floozies."

He had the same lawyer as Chaplin, Jerry Geisler. Known as "Hollywood's Lawyer," Geisler was the first and often the last line of defense in the most celebrated scrapes and matrimonial scraps in Hollywood for many years.

In big time trials, Aggie and I would spell each other, listening to the questions and answers and then dictating them to the rewrite desk. Since neither of us had shorthand, it was wonderful memory training. I got so I could reproduce from only the sketchiest of notes an entire conversation, a talent that came in most handily later. I encountered another Hollywood character between trials, the vicious gossip columnist and Hearst hatchet woman Louella Parsons. She was known as the "Gay Illiterate," which was only half right; illiterate she was, but gaiety was not her strong suit.

One day she telephoned directly with a torrid story about some Hollywood celebrity. Her secretary was out to lunch, so dear Louella undertook to dictate the story herself. Berger ordered me to take it down. As I was typing it, I took the liberty to put it into English. I unsplit a couple of infinitives, changed some words for some that meant what she wanted to say, and made the tenses match.

Louella was furious. She even complained to the chief, William Randolph Hearst, who issued an edict that Miss Parsons' literary efforts were not to be tampered with in future. It was certainly the only time my name was ever mentioned at San Simeon, where the great chief took an active interest in his newspapers, probably to make sure the name of Orson Welles, who had so devastatingly portrayed him in "Citizen Kane" never appeared in one of them. It never did.

First editions of all his papers were flown to San Simeon, and by mid-morning the air was alive with the sound of teletype messages, "suggestions" from the Chief.

It also was important to pay attention to the various Hearst pet causes. The New England Anti-Vivisection Society was one of them, and I once was assigned to write a serious story about the keynote speaker at an Anti-Vivisection Conference (the PETA of the day). The speaker explained, to rapturous applause, how he managed to rid his home of ants. It seems he singled out the head ant and made a deal: he would leave ant delicacies out behind his garage daily, if the ants would agree to stay out of his house. Both sides apparently kept the bargain.

We also had to pay close attention to the doings of any of Marion Davies' relatives. She was Hearst's mistress, loyal to the end. Marion had a sister, Rose Davies, who wrote songs, and many a Hearst reporter wrote stories about her latest opus, always introduced with nationwide flair, and always quickly forgotten.

Another Hearst favorite was the evangelist Aimee Semple McPherson, possibly because she had been the object of one of the scoops of the century by the *Herald-Express* and through it, the entire Hearst empire.

Aimee, or "Sister" as she was known to her enormous flock, was the first famous radio minister. For three decades she ruled over an enormous flock from her Angelus Temple. Aimee was a civic leader, a tourist attraction, and a dispenser of food baskets to the needy in the hardest days of the Depression. My family got a couple and very useful they were.

In her youth, in the Roaring '20s, Aimee had a fondness for young, stalwart lovers, somewhat in the manner of Russia's Catherine the Great. Her first husband, Mr. Semple, died in 1910; Mr. McPherson, after a 1921 divorce, disappeared into the mists of history, and she was married and divorced several times. She usually parked the stud of the moment on her payroll as a "radio operator." One May day in 1926, Aimee and her current operator were canoodling on the sands of Santa Monica beach, when they apparently—this is conjecture, of course—decided to seek privacy, leaving their beach blanket behind.

In a short time, Aimee was missed and presumed drowned. Huge crowds of her believers gathered at the beach to pray for her rescue. Divers were sent into the surf in an attempt to recover her body. It was banner headline stuff for days.

When Aimee came up for air—again conjecture—she must have discovered that her "disappearance" was the object of considerable attention. What to do?

Aimee was next heard from in the desert about 100 miles east of Los Angeles, where she flagged down a passing motorist, and claimed she had been kidnapped and held in a dingy cottage until she made her escape. She had been walking for miles, she related.

The fact that Aimee was clad in a stylish dress and high-heeled shoes which showed no signs of wear, let alone a dusty desert trek, cast some doubt on her story.

Her rescuers took her to the nearest village, where, Hearst luck would have it, an *Evening Herald* reporter happened to be passing through. He telephoned the story of how Aimee, as the *Herald* put it, "disappeared into the ocean, and miraculously reappeared in the desert," and then had the wit to offer to drive Aimee back to civilization, ensuring that no rival news organization would get its hands on her for hours.

The authorities severely scolded Aimee—a diver had lost his life in the "rescue" attempts—but she resumed her evangelical career with barely a missed beat.

In September 1944, Aimee died on a visit to Oakland, and when the word came over the wire, I was dispatched along with a photographer to see how the news was absorbed by the congregation. When we arrived at the Temple we found pandemonium. People were muttering in tongues, rolling about on the floor, waddling about on their knees and gesturing wildly. So many photographic riches were available that the photographer took some time to choose the best. And while he pondered his best angle, I dropped to my knees and began to interview a chap who was rolling over and over. I asked him how he felt about Sister's death.

He stopped rolling immediately. "Sister is dead?" he asked, and as I assured him, the word spread about the room and all the antics stopped. It appeared that we had blundered into a normal prayer session, and so soon as the news spread, the parishioners sat down primly on chairs to absorb it. The pictures were ruined, of course, and the photographer never forgave me for breaking up the photographic maneuvers.

And I did a story about Seabiscuit, the wonder horse soon after his last race, and after a career that won the hearts of America, twice: once in history, and today, in a book and a film.

And I wrote about a piano player who was just starting to sing a little named Nat (King) Cole. In 1936 he had moved from Chicago to Los Angeles where he formed the group that became the King Cole Trio. In 1943, he recorded his first national hit record, "Straighten Up and Fly Right," which was based on one of his father's sermons and on a traditional black folk tale.

And then I turned 18, draft age, and the Army summoned. Berger, I am proud to say, took the news very hard. He told the Army that he could not spare me, which cut absolutely no ice with the military, which had set my induction date.

Reconciled, Berger asked: "Why didn't they draft you before?"

"Because I wasn't old enough," I said. Berger had forgotten. It was probably the best compliment I ever received.

4.
SHANGHAIED

I did my best by the Army, and the Army did even better by me. I learned soldiering in Arkansas that would give me an edge in the future as a war correspondent. I went to Counter-Intelligence School in Texas which came in handy in foreign corresponding. When I was sufficiently trained, the Army shipped me to New York to catch a boat to go overseas where the war was.

I got a 24-hour pass to spend in New York before the ship sailed, and I was bowled over by the Big Apple. The very sidewalks throbbed with energy and nourished my passion for the performing arts. Broadway really was a Great White Way with maybe 40 theaters, offering plays from Shakespeare to Kaufman and Hart, and musicals without echo-chamber miking. (If they had ever hung one of those modern mikes on Ethel Merman she would have blown out all the lights on the Eastern seaboard.)

When I boarded the ship the next day for what turned out to be a 27-day passage to India, I knew that as soon as this war was over I was going to New York and try to make it there. The saying was already current that if you could make it in New York you could make it any-where, but at the time I was interested in only the first goal.

Seasickness out of the way (only 24 hours) it was an idyllic voyage with no sign of the war except at the entrance of the Suez Canal where dozens of ships had been sunk, the tips of their masts sticking out above water.

In India, then undivided into today's separate nations of India, Paki-stan and Bangladesh, the British Raj still ruled, although its glory had been considerably dimmed. Nevertheless, the memsahibs, in a gesture of Anglo-American friendship, frequently invited us untutored colo-nials to tea, an ordeal much more frightening to me than the Japanese enemy.

India was immense, sprawling and complicated, with a bewildering history, magnificent monuments, a brilliant, highly educated upper class and enormous, dispiriting, inescapable poverty. Beggars abounded, women followed cows with outstretched cupped hands hoping to catch droppings which were used as fuel for cooking stoves. The strong smell of cooking oil and burning cow dung hung over the cities.

At night, millions of people unrolled their mats and bedded down in the parks, the city squares, the railroad stations, the sidewalks. These were not "homeless" people in the modern sense of the addicted or afflicted; most had jobs, but sent everything they earned home to the villages to their families, not retaining enough to rent even a hovel.

India repelled; India attracted. There was a fascination about the place that fueled a desire to at least attempt to unravel some of its mys-teries, to find the secret of its spirit of endurance.

Of course, I had no idea at the time that in 20 years or so I would return as the Associated Press Bureau Chief in India, with responsibil-ity for news coverage of all the countries from Iran to Thailand.

And then the war ended, without me firing a shot in anger, and the Army sent me to Shanghai, then perhaps the most exotic place on earth. Shanghai was known as the Paris of the Orient, but even the war-rav-aged city put Paris in the shade. The food was particularly fabulous,

Russian, Armenian, German, French, British afternoon tea, and of course the best Chinese restaurants in the world.

Shanghai also was the hub of the postwar intrigue, as the forces of the Nationalists, led by Chiang Kai-shek, the biggest pirate and thief in modern history—the Marcoses couldn't touch him—an exasperating, prevaricating thoroughly unreliable specimen.

Chiang was hunkered down in Nanking, where he basked in the undying support of the powerful China Lobby in the United States, led by *Time-Life* founder Henry Luce, who had been born in China, and a number of strong senators.

Chiang's rival, and the eventual victor in the civil war soon to erupt, was Mao Tse-tung, who remained with his forces in the north. Mao's right hand, Chou En-lai, probably the best and brightest of the lot, had an office in Shanghai, which he shared with Madame Sun Yat-sen (Ching Ling Soong), the darling of the Communist Revolution, and sister of the celebrated Madame Chiang (May-Ling Soong), which made the coming struggle into something of a family affair.

A third Soong sister, Ai-Ling, married China's richest man, H.H. Kung. In the succinct saying of the time: One sister loved money (Madame Kung), one loved power (Madame Chiang) and one loved China (Madame Sun).

The China over which their civil war was brooding was at its low point in a long and fabled history. Ravaged by nearly 10 years of Japanese aggression, still burdened with Foreign enclaves in Shanghai and elsewhere, China's poverty made India's look like prosperity. People dropped dead of starvation in the streets. Famine reigned in the countryside. In Shanghai when the temperature dropped below even 40, hundreds would freeze to death. Their bodies had been so weakened by malnutrition they had no resistance.

Amidst all this, a gay and glittering social scene flourished.

On my second day in town I bumped into a reporter I had known in L.A. He asked me where I was going and I said I was on my way to report to my counter-intelligence unit. He said he was part of a group being formed to publish a Shanghai edition of the Army newspaper *Stars and Stripes*. "Come with me," he said, and I did.

We went to the office of the soon-to-be *Stars and Stripes*, and he introduced me to the editor. "You are now a member of my staff," said the editor. I protested that I had not yet reported to my unit. "I'll fix that," he said, and he did. The press was powerful there, too. Eventually I did both jobs.

The *Stars and Stripes* Shanghai editor had assembled an extraordinary staff from the ranks of the Army and the Marines. There was an editor of the *National Geographic* (for whom I later wrote), the editor of the *Sporting News*, and other top notch editors, reporters and rewrite men from Philadelphia, Washington, Newark, Chicago and Salt Lake City.

The last was Jack Anderson, who became my roommate, and who sat around the room night after night announcing that when he got out of the Army he intended to go to Washington and become a famous columnist. I countered by stating that I intended to head for Manhattan and land a job doing I knew not what.

For the *Stripes* I covered the visits of major bigwigs, including General Eisenhower, who stiffed a press conference with the civilian reporters to spend considerable time with Jack and me. He wanted to grill us on the status of military morale, and the seriousness of the "Go Home" demonstrations that were beginning to swell in the ranks of the civilian Army.

I was attached to the party of General George Marshall, the most outstanding man I ever reported on, during the first of his many forays into China in fruitless attempts to patch up a truce between Chiang and Mao.

A man of steely countenance and towering intellect, General Marshall had a reputation for suffering fools not at all. It was therefore even more amazing that during a conversation we had standing under the wing of an airplane, when I blurted out: "General, we must solve this China problem," he did not treat me with the contempt I probably deserved. I was 19, and now knew everything.

Instead the General responded with words that guided me throughout my reporting life. "Young man," he said, "there are problems in foreign affairs that must be solved. And there are problems that must be left alone to wear themselves out. Statesmanship is the ability to recognize the difference."

I covered war crimes trials of the Japanese occupiers of China, and the simmering Chinese civil war, and boxing matches and the Shanghai Symphony, and a host of lighter things, the Rickshaw Derby, the Rice Bowl football game between the Army and the Navy that had four All-Americans in it, even a golf tournament.

However, I was afraid I made my most lasting mark on the *Stars and Stripes* through sheer carelessness. The *Stripes* was published in the offices of a famed newspaper, the *Shanghai Evening Post and Mercury*. We inherited many of its typesetters, most Chinese with rudimentary English who followed copy letter by letter.

As a result, one staff member was assigned each night to make a midnight check on the newspaper before it went to press. One night, when it was my turn, I carefully read the stories and even the photo captions, and checked the usual trouble spots. All looked fine, so I signed off on the paper.

Unfortunately, I had not thought to scrutinize the headlines. On the back page, atop a story about the displaced persons in Europe, was a headline intended to read: POPULATION SHIFT TROUBLES EUROPE. Unfortunately, the typesetter had left the "F" out of SHIFT. The result was a very nasty looking word, in 48 point type. I had missed it, and the members of the staff have never once neglected to remind me at our various reunions.

Then, having soared to the rank of staff sergeant (although us Stripers never wore rank insignia or anything that resembled official uniform), and having collected considerable knowledge and experience that would prove useful in years to come, the Army decided it could dispense with my services. Free at last, I determined to proceed with my plan. I was honorably discharged at the same base in Southern California where I had been sworn in a couple of years before. Upon discharge, the Army presented its ex-soldiers with $300, although they did not trust us with it all at once. It was doled out in $100 increments. I took my first hundred, and with my soon-to-be wife Betty, bought two one-way tickets to New York on the Greyhound bus. I had met Betty in Shanghai where we were both in the Army. Staff Sgt. Jim Becker and Staff Sgt. Betty Hanson seemed destined to meet.

In New York, I picked out the Associated Press, where I knew nobody, because it was the world's largest news agency, and I presumed rightly that it would have the world's largest number of jobs. I marched into the AP's offices at 50 Rockefeller Plaza stone cold. I had no degree. In fact I never spent a day at a university until I was 48, except to make a speech, and then in London. The only reference I had was a letter from Jack Berger, who had kindly expanded the period of my employment with him. I had just turned 20, and thought it was wise to add a few years on my own; it was many years before that got straightened out at the AP.

I must have had a presence. Some years later, a Filipino columnist wrote: "Jim Becker is the kind of guy who wherever he goes leaves friends and non-friends alike fairly stunned by the force of his personality, like a dynamite fisherman in Manila Bay." His words, not mine, but it may explain what followed.

I was introduced to a wonderful man named Joe Wing, who did the hiring for AP. We talked for a couple minutes about this and that, and then Joe asked me if I knew anything about sports. I said I did, and he hired me on the spot, at a salary beyond my wildest dreams, $82.50 a week.

I asked Joe when he wanted me to report for duty. "How about tomorrow morning?" he asked, and I said I thought I could manage that.

A seasoned war reporter, now I was a sportswriter, and on the threshold of the magic $100 mark. All that remained was the foreign correspondent bit (I was to be the youngest, 24, in AP history), and the columnist thing, which came some 20 years later in Hawaii. That lay ahead, but now it was time to try to make it in Manhattan.

46

5.
BREAKING IN

New York in the immediate postwar years was a sportswriter's heaven. Three of the 16 major league baseball teams played there: the Brooklyn Dodgers, with their field that jumped with joy; the New York Giants, with a grand history and a quirky ballpark where Babe Ruth played his first seasons as a Yankee; and the New York Yankees, with their storied stadium and majestic manner. Their respective radio voices were Red Barber, the model of them all, Frankie Frisch ("oh, those bases on balls") and Mel Allen ("how about that").

College basketball teams prepped all season for their date on one of the doubleheaders at Madison Square Garden, also home to championship boxing. There were teams in both professional football leagues; one of the six National Hockey League teams in the days of skill before the Designated Thug; indoor track meets where runners pursued in vain the four-minute mile; tennis at Forest Hills, and golf tournaments that drew Hogan, Nelson, Snead and the putting genius Bobby Locke of South Africa. New York had it all.

And one dank April day in 1947, a very black man in a blindingly white home uniform of the Brooklyn Dodgers walked out of the dugout carrying an odd-looking mitt. It was Jackie Robinson, a middle infielder carrying a first baseman's mitt, who was to make his debut as the Dodgers' first baseman, and incidentally break the color barrier that had disfigured the game for half a century.

It is difficult to imagine today the atmosphere in which Robinson made his breakthrough. Racial segregation was the law of the land in the South, and the unwritten law elsewhere. Blacks in their own country could not eat in restaurants, stay in hotels, shop in stores or live in certain areas. Having grown up among them I knew first hand this humiliating, back-of-the-bus existence so many of our fellow citizens were forced to endure: Zelda duBois and I were once asked to leave the dance floor in a Los Angeles night club where Louis Armstrong was headlining. No mixed dancing was allowed.

And definitely no mixed ball playing.

I drew the assignment as part of the AP team covering Jackie Robinson's first pro game because I had seen him play in his college days at U.C.L.A. My job was to talk to him before and after the game and write what we called a "sidebar" story.

Jackie Robinson was the greatest all-round athlete I ever saw. You could invent a game and within 15 minutes he would be the best at it. At UCLA he was the first athlete ever to letter in four sports in one year. In his senior year, he led the nation in yards per carry in football, led the Pacific Coast Conference in scoring in basketball, ran the sprints and broke the long jump record (set by his brother Matt, who was second to Jesse Owens in the 1936 Berlin Olympics to the further chagrin of Hitler), often participated in track meets and baseball games on the same day for the L.A. Bruins, and won two tennis tournaments which in Southern California in the 1940s was no mean achievement; that's where the tennis players were. A gifted runner and ferocious defender, he led the nation one season in ground gaining and was the first black to play in the East-West Shrine All-Star football game in San Francisco.

But Robinson was never completely comfortable at UCLA. He had a long commute to the campus in Westwood, then a lily-white community. UCLA had only a few handfuls of black students, and although they included his future wife, Rachel, and the future Mayor of Los Angeles, Tom Bradley, he felt increasingly shut out of campus activities. He heard racial slurs from supporters of some visiting teams.

Finally he lost interest and did not finish his degree, even though he lacked just a few credits.

Out of school, barred from major professional sports, Robinson signed a contract to go to Hawaii and play for one of the four semi-pro teams in the Islands. He played 18 games, the last few while hampered by a gimpy knee, and sailed for home on December 5, 1941, two days before the Japanese bombed Pearl Harbor and propelled the United States into war. Robinson was an Army officer in the war, where he also played a pioneering role. He refused to move to the back of the bus on an Army post.

So in 1947, this magnificent 28-year-old athlete had taken the field to carry the banner of decency and dignity and humanity for us all. Jackie Robinson's victory in this noble enterprise was his and his alone; his defeat would have been our defeat, all of ours. Defeat was not of course an option for Jackie Robinson. He had a Churchillian inner strength, a powerful intellect and a will of steel.

He would need it all. His road to the major leagues had not exactly been paved with good intentions. Branch Rickey, the general manager of the Dodgers, had stepped forward and signed Robinson and then promoted him to the major league club. He had sent Robinson to the Brooklyn farm team in Montreal for the 1946 season, where Jackie had batted .349 and was voted Most Valuable Player. Rickey then made sure the Dodger players watched Robinson in action during spring training, before he announced his promotion to the big club. It didn't work.

No sooner was Robinson made an official Brooklyn Dodger than a number of his teammates drew up a petition of protest; they said they did not want to play with him.

Although the captain of the team—Kentuckian PeeWee Reese, short-stop and superior human being—was conspicuous by his absence, a number of players called on their manager, Leo Durocher, and presented the petition to him.

Leo Durocher was the most foul-mouthed man I ever heard, which is saying something, and he did not spare the language when he addressed the protesters. Here is the gist of his remarks:

"I would play an elephant if he would help me win. And this guy ain't no elephant. He is a better ball player than any man in this room. And furthermore, there are a lot more where he came from, and they are better ball players than any of us, too. Now stick that petition, and get out of my room."

Those of us covering the story knew about the petition. We knew because the Brooklyn team officials told us. They wanted us to know, because some of them, and some of us, were fresh back from fighting fascism and organized racial hatred at the level of insanity, and were keen to fight it at home.

All of us were determined to avoid the media feeding frenzy that would make Robinson's burden even heavier. All we wanted was an even chance; Robinson would do the rest.

Life was tough enough for any rookie in those days, let alone a black one; he was taking a job away from a long-time friend and teammate. So the five or six of us with dressing room duty made sure we talked to some of the veteran players before we descended on Robinson, both before and after the game.

And the writers doing the main story generally hit the theme that the Brooklyn Dodgers opened the 1947 season today against the Boston Braves, and, oh, by the way, a black man played first base.

Robinson went hitless in the game, and I asked him after if it was because he was nervous, and he said, no, it was because Johnny Sain, the ace of the Boston staff, was pitching.

Writers kept the same tone throughout the season. I wrote the review of the sports year for AP, and it was published in the annual anthology of Best Sports Stories. It was my first time between hard covers; I was just 21. Although I knew full well that Robinson's entry into the major leagues was the event that would ring down the halls of time, I put it in the 11th paragraph, deliberately.

Most visiting writers were of the same mind, excluding one redneck from Cincinnati. He was one of those who hide a lack of talent under a barrage of figures, in a style described by Red Smith, "that isn't writing, that's arithmetic." The redneck described all of us, collectively, as "low-down nigger-loving Jew Commie bastards." Dick Young of the *New York Daily News* bless his memory, knocked him out cold.

The St. Louis writers tipped us to the fact that the Cardinals were threatening to strike rather than play against Robinson. The Commissioner, Ford Frick, told them he would banish them all from baseball for life, so they played, although one of them, Enos Slaughter, attempted to cut Robinson's leg off in a play at first base. (I had dinner with Slaughter just before he died, and he denied it, but Robinson could show you the scar.)

Foul as Slaughter's act was, he was a gentleman compared to the Philadelphia Phillies, under manager Ben Chapman, who threw at Robinson at every bat, tried to spike him at every opportunity and hurled vile abuse that could be heard in the press box. In response, between innings, PeeWee Reese walked quietly over to Robinson and stood for a moment with his hand on his teammate's shoulder. It was a simple gesture, hardly dramatic, but it still sends chills down my spine when I recall it.

Shortly after, Dixie Walker, right fielder, cleanup hitter, and "peoples' cherce," who had demanded to be traded rather than play with Robinson, came to see Branch Rickey, and said:

"Forget what I said about a trade, Mr. Rickey. This nigrah can play."

And then he added the ultimate ball player's compliment: "We can win with him."

And to his eternal credit, Rickey replied: "No, Dixie, after the season you're gone." And he was: traded to the Pittsburgh Pirates, then the pits, for a left-handed pitcher who never won a game for the Dodgers.

The Dodgers did win, and played one of the most dramatic seven-game World Series ever, against the New York Yankees, a series memorable for its fourth game in which Bill Bevens of the Yankees pitched eight and two-thirds innings of no-hit ball, only to lose the game when pinch hitter Cookie Lavagetto doubled off the right field wall to score two runners who had walked. In the sixth game, an obscure Brooklyn outfielder named Al Gionfriddo caught up with a Joe DiMaggio blast at the 415-foot mark and gloved it. DiMaggio was approaching second base when the ball came down in Gionfriddo's glove. DiMaggio angrily kicked at the dirt, the only time anyone ever saw the great man display emotion on the field.

Robinson was named Rookie of the Year. He had kicked the door of major league baseball down with his skill and his manner, with grace and dignity. He had not sought the role of social pioneer; all he wanted was to be a ball player. He told me once, "I can hardly wait for some umpire to kick me out of a game," in other words, to treat him like just another ball player.

Fifty years on, Betty and I were taking one of our many baseball trips with the Jay Buckley organization. Jay hauls bus loads of baseball fans to games all over the country all summer long. One year they gave us a calendar, with each month illustrated by a photo of a famous ball park.

We didn't open the calendar to its center spread until we got home. It was a two-by-three-foot photo montage of Jackie Robinson at bat for the first time in the major leagues. In the background was the Press Box. Betty looked at the photo. "That's you," she said, pointing to the AP contingent in the box. "I still remember ironing that damn shirt." And so it was. Jackie and me.

6.
THE ANTI-RED BARON

Late in 1949 old Army roommate Jack Anderson called me from Washington where he was the top leg-man for Drew Pearson, the reigning Capitol columnist of the day. (He wrote the column called: Washington Merry-Go-Round and he was a power in the land.)

Jack said that Drew Pearson was planning on retiring soon, and he suggested I come down and join him in writing the column. So I flew down to Washington and spent a day with Drew and Jack, talking about it, but in the end we all agreed amicably that it was not a perfect fit. (My career with AP was thriving, and I would soon be a war correspondent in Korea.) Jack drove me to the airport for my return flight to New York. My flight was delayed a couple of hours as flights often were in those days. Also delayed was the flight to Milwaukee of the junior Senator from Wisconsin, one Joseph McCarthy.

McCarthy was anything but a power in the land at the time. In fact, a press club poll had recently named him the worst Senator in the United

States. (There were only 96 at the time, but it was still a title not to be cherished.) McCarthy was widely considered a political accident who was not long for the Senate. He had no issue. Privately he was known as the Senator for one of the big soft drink companies. Sugar rationing was still in effect and the company in question wanted a larger allocation. McCarthy obligingly tacked a rider onto every possible bill granting the company more sugar, and it would dutifully be kicked out in committee.

Jack, young in the Washington news gathering game was anxious to acquire sources, and McCarthy was keen to be so acquired, so they had become professional acquaintances, newsman to possible news source. Spotting McCarthy at a table in the airport waiting room, Jack joined him, and introduced me. The Senator was a lively conversationalist, especially when he had two newsmen, one from AP New York and the other from Washington, for an audience. We talked of this and that, sports, about our Army service, very little politics. What I remember so vividly from the hour-long conversation was that the one subject that never came up was Communism. Nary a word.

The Senator had not yet discovered the issue which he would ride into the dictionary where the word McCarthyism eventually found a place as "the use of indiscriminate, often unfounded, accusations, sensationalism, inquisitorial investigative methods, etc.," and it never occurred to me to ask him about it.

I have to admit I liked him, but I did notice something strange about his drinking habits. Here was the Senator from one of the few states in our union that produces potable beer, and the Senator from Wisconsin was drinking Ballentine ale, manufactured in New York and barely fit to drink anywhere. (I haven't seen any for years and presume it has gone down the drain.)

McCarthyism was born a few months later when the Senator was fulfilling a speaking engagement at the Wheeling, West Virginia., Womens' Club. He was reading the standard Republican Party foreign policy speech of that period that implied that the "loss" of China to Communism—Mao's forces had just finished conquering the Chinese mainland—was due to the machinations of "pinkos and fellow travelers" in the State Department and government agencies. As the speech had been given dozens of times before by other Republican Party speakers, it did not exactly grip the audience so the Senator apparently decided to jazz it up by elevating "pinkos and fellow travelers" into card-carrying Communists, and, perhaps carried away by the sound of his own voice or a pre-lunch cocktail or two, declared that he held in his hand a list of such Communists in Government employ. (A list that was never produced.) That went down well, and an AP reporter in the house put it on the wires. The national press descended upon McCarthy at his next stop, and the witch hunt carried on from there.

McCarthy had his issue in that paranoid time of Cold War and Communist expansion. To Jack's eternal credit, he wrote the first book exposing McCarthy's unscrupulous methods, but it was nearly four years until the reign of terror ended, in McCarthy's censure by the Senate, and many careers were ruined in the interim. There were even trials of alleged Communists in Hawaii, which I reported.

But as my assignments took me elsewhere, I never saw McCarthy again.

✳✳✳

As time went by, I got kicked upstairs to AP Newsfeatures, a more sedate scene two floors above the hubbub of the daily news. Though still immersed in sports, I began to branch out a bit. I interviewed a famous Miss America who hated the job. "The best thing about being Miss America is that after a year you aren't," I wrote. And I covered some opera singers and some personalities who were emerging from the new-fangled thing called television.

I had a desk in a room full of writers, some of whom were known to spend a week crafting the opening sentence of an article. I might add that often it was worth the time spent.

And it was into this serene existence that Baron X, a redoubtable Freedom Fighter, intruded. The Cold War had just begun to cast its chill. Anti-Communism was the mood, which made the time ripe for the anti-Red Baron.

Of course Baron X was not his real name, but that was the one he was using when he sprang into prominence via a front page story under the double-decker headline and a six-column photo showing the back of his head in *The New York Journal-American*, a now-defunct and little-lamented newspaper.

The byline on the story was By Cholly Knickerbocker, and that was not his real name either. The writer was Igor Cassini, the less-talented of the Cassini brothers, the other being Oleg, dress designer to Jackie Kennedy Onassis among others.

As their first names indicated, the Cassinis claimed descent from Russian aristocrats and had good contacts in anti-Communist circles.

Igor had been steered to the Baron, who professed to be a leader in the underground movement fighting against Soviet occupation of the Baltic states: Latvia, Lithuania and Estonia.

The Baron was one of the leaders of this underground Army that was harassing Soviet troops in their homelands. With a price on his head he had escaped by submarine to the West, where he hoped to garner support and money for his cause. His tale of sabotage, propaganda and hairbreadth escapes made compelling reading.

The fact that the Baron would allow only the back of his head to be photographed was explained; he feared assassination by Soviet agents if his name or face were revealed.

The afternoon of the Baron's exposure, I was crafting away at my desk in what was known as the Writers' Room at AP Newsfeatures. My desk was between that of the AP science writer Alton Blakeslee and our book critic, Bill Rogers, a 1920s Paris pal of Hemingway and Fitzgerald, who had given up writing books and turned to reviewing them.

My telephone rang. It was Jack Anderson. As he had promised back in our Army days in Shanghai, Jack had gone to Washington upon his discharge from the Army to begin his ambition to become a "famous columnist." Jack was now the right hand man of Drew Pearson, whose column, Washington Merry-go-Round, was very big-league.

Jack told me that Drew Pearson had sent him to New York to get the full story of Baron X and the guerrilla fighters in the Baltic States. Jack said he had found the Baron easily enough, after all, that was why the Baron had come to New York: to be found by the influential press.

But, Jack said, this wily underground fighter was refusing to be interviewed in any public place where Soviet agents could get at him. No restaurant, no hotel room, not even a Central Park bench. The Baron demanded neutral ground.

At the time Betty and I had a rent-controlled apartment on East 43rd Street in Manhattan.

Jack asked me if he could interview the Baron in our apartment. I said sure, and we set 7 p.m. as the time.

When I came home I told Betty that Jack was coming over to interview the Baron X whose story had featured so prominently in the *Journal-American*. As the appointed time neared, Betty went into the kitchen and began preparing a snack for the guests.

The Baron was the first to arrive. He had in tow an emaciated female who he introduced to us as a Danish princess. She was laconic, even for a Dane, and sat quietly in the corner throughout the ensuing events. The Baron was a bundle of activity, on the other hand. He peered carefully behind all the pictures in the living room, obviously hunting for hidden microphones.

Satisfied that the place was bug-free, he sat down. Jack arrived on the dot, and sat down to begin the interview.

The Baron obliged with the details of his thrilling escape from Soviet forces via submarine, and began recounting various guerrilla battles in the mountains and harrowing chases through the streets of cities with exotic names.

He was in full flow when Betty entered with a tray full of cheese and crackers.

She stopped in her tracks and eyed Baron X. He looked equally intently at her. Then Betty spoke.

"Hello, Ed," she said.

"Hello, Betty," he replied.

It turned out that they had gone to West High School in Minneapolis together. Eight million people in New York, and he winds up in the apartment of the only one who knew him when.

For, as you will have gathered, he was not a Baron, X or otherwise, nor a freedom fighter, nor an underground warrior, nor a Baltic patriot, nor anti-Communist crusader.

He was in fact Ed Tkach of Minneapolis, Minnesota, a con man by profession, who had never been out of the United States in his life, and had recently escaped from the Minnesota Hospital for the Criminally Insane.

And so, before our astonished eye, Baron X became Ed Tkach. He and Betty went through their high school year book and reminisced. "Did you remember Miss Wanda Orton's Shakespeare class?" Betty later remembered that Ed had called himself Count in high school; Baron was a bit of a demotion.

This went on for several minutes, while Jack and I ate the cheese and crackers, and then the screw slipped in Ed's befuddled mind, and he became Baron X, Freedom Fighter again.

Whereupon Jack and I threw him out in the street, and the princess, too. We waited until the next day to blow the Baron's cover because we wanted the *Journal*'s main rival, *The New York Post*, to get the story. Anything to make Igor look like an idiot.

Hence fate had one more nasty shock in store for this Minnesota hoaxer.

The next morning I was at my desk when the telephone rang on the next desk, the one occupied by our book critic. I answered it.

"Is Bill Rogers there?" asked a voice.

I said he was home reading books and could I take a message.

"Well, maybe you can help me," the man said. He explained he was from one of the leading publishing houses, and he had in his office at this very moment the fellow who was featured in the *Journal-American*, Baron X, the Baltic Freedom Fighter. He said he and the Baron were discussing an advance on a book about the Baron's adventures.

"I figured you newspaper guys know these things, and I thought Bill might have some inside scoop on this man."

"I doubt Bill can help you," I said, "but you happen to be talking to the only man in New York whose wife went to high school with the guy."

And I told all.

The man was relieved. "You know, I was darn near ready to write the man a check, if he had asked for something like $5,000," the man at the publishing house explained. "But he asked for only $500, and that made me decide to check up on him. Who would write a book for a $500 advance?"

Who, indeed.

PART TWO–
A FONDNESS FOR WAR

7.
EMBEDDED

War again intervened, as it would periodically for the next half-century. War is the ultimate challenge, personally and professionally, and God help me, I developed a fondness for it.

Joe Wing, the astute editor who had hired me for AP after a couple of minutes of small talk, sent me one of his famous yellow pad notes that read, "See me please." I still have it.

I saw him, and he informed me that I was now a war correspondent. Some months before, the North Koreans had invaded South Korea, an American protectorate, and the war had seesawed until General MacArthur sent his United Nations forces all the way north to the Yalu River, the boundary between Korea and China. Now the conflict entered a dangerous phase; Chinese armies were pouring into Korea creating what MacArthur called a "whole new war."

Fresh war correspondents were needed, and I had been selected to be one.

"When do I go?" I asked. "Saturday," said Joe, and handed me a one-way airline ticket to Tokyo. It was Thursday. "I don't even have a passport," I said. "Sign here," said Joe, "and you have one now." I did. The AP can move when it wants.

Away I went, to begin what turned out to be decades, off and on, of War and Foreign Corresponding, fulfilling the second stage of the three-stage plan I laid out in seventh grade at Foshay, in South Central L.A.

When I arrived in Korea, two veteran correspondents, Don Whitehead and Hal Boyle, gave me the only advice I needed: "Never forget your communications. A story is no good unless you can get it out."

Boyle added, "Always wear shorts to keep the fart stains off your long johns." He explained that if I intended to be a real war correspondent, and not one who lolls around headquarters, be it Paris or Saigon or Baghdad, baths would come few and far between.

I was quickly to learn the joys of bathing with a helmet full of cold water, in zero temperatures, and once went 27 days without a shower. Finally cleansed, I burned my entire wardrobe and began with a fresh outfit.

Over the years since Korea, communications have changed dramatically. War corresponding hasn't.

There are two ways to cover a war. One is to be *embedded*, a term that has recently taken on a sinister connotation among conspiracy theorists. To be embedded means to live with a unit, ideally a division, move with it, advance with it, retreat with it if necessary, to become such a part of it that you assume the aspect of a fly on the wall. Soldiers soon forget you are there and talk freely. You get the same briefings commanders get. Everybody knows you are not going to rush off and reveal anything of military value to the enemy, because the people who get killed as a result could include you.

This is the way to get the feel and flavor of warfare. It was Ernie Pyle's way.

The other way is to roam around the battle area, looking for random shortages of equipment (always a good story) or ammunition, atrocities, even occasional successes.

I've done both. I found the inevitable shortages and helped to get them fixed. I found and reported atrocities, from Suwon in Korea to the mountains of Lebanon. Still, with either method, a reporter gets only part of the big picture; a calamity in one place can be balanced by a brilliant maneuver in another. It takes writers at headquarters to collect dispatches from reporters in the field to make sense of them. Even then we don't always get it right. The important thing is to tell the truth as you see it.

I have written at least half a million words—maybe a million; who counts?—from war zones in my lifetime, and I never once wrote a word that I didn't believe was true. Nor have I ever been asked to, by my bosses, or by the military.

I have been lied to. I have been wrong, but I always believed I was right when I wrote, and in the vast majority of cases, I was.

But if the way to get a story hasn't changed, the ways to get it out have changed beyond recognition of the Ernie Pyles, the Don Whiteheads, the Hal Boyles. This may be a good thing and it may not, depending on the caliber of reporter. "Rubbish in, rubbish out" still goes.

Communications were unbelievably primitive in Korea. I was embedded with the Marines at a time when we were totally surrounded by Chinese troops. It was an unnerving sight: brown-clad figures tiny to the naked eye swarming over the mountains to our right and left, scurrying south to try to cut off our retreat, looking like colonies of ants whose hill had been kicked over.

The Marines were fighting their way out—the units on both sides had collapsed and then disappeared—or as the Marines liked to say, "We are advancing in a different direction." I love those guys.

The Marines had the flimsiest of communications with the outside world, and there was no intention to use them to send the dispatches of the seven correspondents accompanying the Division. In fact, the Marines put us all to work as perimeter guards. We seven were called in and issued rifles. "We're non-combatants," one correspondent explained. "You are now honorary Marines," was the reply. "Report for duty."

Helicopters dropped in regularly to deliver huge containers of water. The Marines used most of the water to make coffee, without which the Marines cannot exist.

I once suggested that I be issued a small quantity of water to brush my teeth. "Brush them in coffee," I was instructed. It is an acquired taste, I'm afraid.

The helicopters took out our seriously wounded. This gave me an idea. I wrote my stories on an Olivetti portable parked on the hood of a Jeep, and stuck them in the shirt pockets of the seriously wounded men, with a little note attached: "Dear doctor or nurse: If you find this please telephone the nearest Associated Press office."

The first of my stories to emerge did so in Washington, D.C. The Marine in whose jacket pocket I had placed the story had been flown to the Bethesda Naval Hospital near Washington, and a nurse had called the AP office. All my stories eventually surfaced.

That was an extreme case, but communications at the best of times in Korea ranged from the briefly adequate to the truly awful. Reporters were forced to dictate their dispatches to their offices over land lines strung all over the peninsula. The voice quality deteriorated with every mile, and every switchboard, from Division, to Corps (code-named *Jackson*) to Army headquarters (code-named *Scotch*).

One day I got a call from AP headquarters and Dick Applegate, the superb UP reporter said, "There is a man standing at the bottom of a well talking through a handkerchief who wants to speak to you."

By Vietnam, the telephone worked, but television cameramen still had to shoot their stuff on film and ship it back to the States for transmission. Still later, when I coordinated the Yom Kippur War in 1973 for Westinghouse Broadcasting out of London, I was able to hook up correspondents on opposite sides by satellite and have them talk to each other on the air. The man with the vastly outnumbered Israeli forces on the Golan Heights said to the reporter with the overwhelming Syrian

Army, "We're half an hour's drive from Damascus, and it is downhill all the way." In the end, they never made that drive as the Israelis drove the Syrians back in the second week of the conflict.

Communications include more than telephones, of course. Planes, helicopters, jeeps, and even taxis are important in getting the story, and getting it out. I say "even taxis" because during one of the earlier Middle East conflicts, Betty and I were sightseeing in Jerusalem, when fighting broke out. The AP decided it wanted me in Beirut, the then-lovely capital city of Lebanon, where the Mediterranean was a stunning shade of blue and the food was beyond fabulous.

No planes were flying between Jerusalem and Beirut, so I stepped outside my hotel in Jerusalem, hailed a taxi and instructed the driver to take me to Beirut. And off we went, on a journey that took all day and half the night, through Amman in Jordan, through the fantastic Roman ruins at Jerash, through Damascus, where there really is a street called Straight, and to the Lebanese border, where we switched taxis, when my original driver chickened out at the sound of gunfire. (Shades of my Dalai Lama pilot.)

The new driver took us down the steep mountain road to Beirut. We were stopped five times at checkpoints manned by villainous-looking bands. Representing competing interests and armed to the clavicles, each of them searched Betty's purse, inspected our passports and waved us on with bemused expressions. They obviously thought we were mad, but when you have a press pass you begin to think you are immortal. Anyway, we made it, the most expensive taxi ride the AP ever paid for. (I rivaled it once in Taiwan, but never surpassed it.)

At the St. George Hotel in Beirut I found the AP photographer Jim Pringle had arrived ahead of me and was concocting martinis in his hotel room bathtub. The Pringle recipe was to pour a case of gin over a block of ice, add a dash of vermouth and stir with the bayonet he always carried for good luck. The resultant mixture wasn't too bad.

Dublin-born and bred, Pringle had a tendency to plant the Irish flag in any premises he occupied anywhere in the world and was an old hand at communications. We had been teamed up in Korea, where we immediately began to suffer from the shortage of jeeps, a chronic condition there, probably because the war was not expected to last so long. "Home by Christmas," was the watchword, but which Christmas was the question.

Pringle's solution was to sneak into the repair shop of a Division motor pool and steal the first jeep he saw. There was a drawback. The jeep apparently had been in the repair shop because it had no brakes. None at all.

Pringle devised a method of stopping the thing by jamming it into reverse, then to first gear, reverse again, jockeying it back and forth until it came to a complete stop.

In an emergency, or when pressed for time, Jim would ram the jeep into a sturdy tree. Years later, I went back to Korea and found that Jim's target trees had grown considerably, but still bore the scars from the collisions.

Having more or less perfected his stopping technique, one day as Jim was driving me along the dusty road behind the front line, we saw a couple of foot-weary soldiers trudging along. Jim decided to offer them a lift. He jammed the jeep into reverse, and we passed the soldiers going backwards. A shift to first gear and we passed them going forward. Another reverse pass, a forward pass, and finally Jim brought the vehicle to a stop alongside the two GIs.

"Want a ride?" he asked them. They thought about it for several moments.

"No thanks," one said, "we'd rather walk."

During a lull in the action, Jim found time to get the jeep repainted, expunging all traces of its original ownership, and to get the brakes repaired. Being Pringle, he neglected to tell me. We were whizzing down the road at his customary pace when Jim suddenly said, "Look! Brakes." And he slammed them on, hurling me knees-first into the dashboard. Like the trees, I still bear the scars.

8.
SHELLING SEOUL

Homer, the world's first War Correspondent, taught all his successors that the news is in the capitals. Homer's headlines came when the Greeks took Troy. The big news from the Peloponnesian War was the capture of Athens by the Spartans.

Alexander conquered Babylon. The Crusaders took—and lost—Jerusalem. The Huns sacked Rome. Napoleon took Moscow and lost an empire. "Like Grant took Richmond" became a part of the language. Liberate Paris, capture Berlin, bomb Tokyo, enter Saigon, storm Baghdad. That's the news.

In Korea the news was Seoul.

Seoul is just south of the 38th parallel, which the North Koreans poured across in late June of 1950. We lost Seoul in the first days of the Korean War, won it back after the Inchon landings in September, and abandoned it for a second time around year's end. After the second retreat from Seoul it appeared to many in the field, and almost everyone at home, that the war in Korea was lost.

The Army seemed to be retreating five miles a day. No sooner had we settled in one place than the order would come to "pack," and move south some more. There seemed to be no particular reason for this as we appeared to have outrun the Chinese advance. It was simply a case of general panic. In fact, what little shooting there was, at least in my area, came from our own people shooting at imaginary targets or occasionally at each other. The regiment on my right and the regiment on my left got into a fairly vigorous fire fight one night and the tracers flying over our position in the middle were a trifle unnerving.

General MacArthur, possibly seeing his unsullied military reputation going down in flames, was dashing off letters to legislators and editors recommending nuclear war, a recommendation the Joint Chiefs of Staff in Washington said would be "the wrong war in the wrong place at the wrong time against the wrong enemy," and you can't get it much more wrong than that.

Enter General Matthew Ridgway, a kind of Patton with tact, a fighting paratrooper general, and a man to whom "pack" was a four-letter word not to be mentioned in his presence.

Ridgway took stock of the gloomy situation and looked around for some leaders who felt the same way he did about mindless retreats.

Ridgway found one in the Third Division, with which I was embedded at the time. The Third held down the left flank of the line, and was currently camped about 50 miles due south of Seoul. It was considered good form, which I seldom followed, to refer to our forces in Korea as "United Nations troops" as we were operating under the flag of the U.N., but the bulk of our effective forces were American, with a stout British Commonwealth Division as our major ally and a smaller force of fierce Turks. It would be at least a year before the South Korean Army did much more than take up space.

The Third Division was led by General Soule, known as "Shorty" to all—he was about five-six. He was a tough-talking, hard-drinking soldier who told me one evening, "I could go back and take Seoul tomorrow if they ordered me to."

I wrote this, and the general's comments were treated with considerable interest and front-page display by editors in America, who had caught the glooms from all the other dispatches they were receiving from the war.

This was just the sort of thing General Ridgway wanted to hear, since the recapture of Seoul was exactly what he had in mind. He knew, too, that the news is in the capitals.

Hence, on a biting cold morning just after dawn in late January, Ridgway personally supervised the kickoff of an offensive driving due north. The first few miles were the hardest. The two hills on either side of the road to Seoul were strongly defended. On the left, a company of the fabled 27th "Wolfhound" Regiment actually made the last recorded bayonet charge to clear their hill. On the right, the Turks took a little longer than anticipated in clearing the enemy off its hill. Due to a communications failure the Turks thought they were expected to kill all the defenders, rather than simply chasing them off, and that naturally took a little longer.

This turned out to be a masking force and the way was pretty much clear for the next few days. Within a week, the troops had gobbled up more than half the distance to Seoul, and we were able to begin including the name of the capital city in dispatches.

A day or two later, Pringle and I were driving our no-longer brakeless jeep up the dusty road to Seoul when we spotted a Third Division jeep parked alongside the road. A colonel was seated in it, and he was talking on his radio mike. We stopped and I asked him what he was doing.

"I've got five tanks out there probing the ground ahead of us," he explained. His name was Tom Dolvin and I was about to give him at least 15 hours of fame. It is customary to send out tank patrols in front of infantry positions, both to check on enemy positions and to draw fire, which gives away the position and number of their guns.

Dolvin picked up the big map on the seat beside him and showed me where his five tanks were operating. "I've got one over here on the right," he said, "and two here on the left, and one checking that minor road there. Oh, and one tank is way up north checking the main road." And he pointed to the spot. It was about 10 miles south of Seoul.

That set off bells. I knew if I could tell the world that we have moved within shelling range of Seoul and fired some rounds into the enemy-held capital city, it would demonstrate to the outside world that instead of cutting and running, this Army was heading north with a purpose. It would signal that the war wasn't lost.

I pointed to the lead tank. "He could hit Seoul from there, couldn't he," I asked Dolvin.

A tank can shoot through a keyhole at a range of a mile or two, but if the gun is elevated, it can easily fire 10 or 12 miles. I had been around armies, even been in one, long enough to know that.

"Sure he can," Dolvin said.

"Well, would you mind shelling Seoul for me?" I asked.

"No problem," said Dolvin, and picked up his radio mike. "Easy Rider One, this is Easy Rider Six," he said. "You know that big town in front of you?"

"Easy Rider Six, this is Easy Rider One," came the reply, loud and clear. "You mean Yong-dong-Po?" Yong-dong-Po is a suburb of Seoul on the south bank of the Han River.

"No, no, no," said Dolvin. "I mean the really big town."

"Say again," said the man in the tank.

"I mean, Sugar Easy Oboe Uncle Love," said Dolvin, using Army phonetics to hide his meaning should the enemy be listening.

"Oh, Seoul," said the man in the tank, blurting it out. "I can't hit any specific target in there."

"Easy Rider One, it's a big place," said Colonel Dolvin. "You can't miss it."

"Roger, Six," said the tanker "Elevating and firing now."

I heard over the radio a series of clump, clump, clumps as the shells winged their way toward the capital.

"Thank you, Colonel," I said, and headed back for one of those dreaded signal corps telephones to ask Jackson to get me Scotch, and he did, and I related the story to AP headquarters. An Army probing force had maneuvered to within range of Seoul, and had shelled the city.

Big stuff, indeed. The *New York Daily News,* then the nation's largest-circulation newspaper, had just two words on its tabloid front page the next day: SEOUL SHELLED. And inside, my story. I wrote that a unit of the Third Division advanced within range of Seoul today and began shelling enemy forces in the capital.

Mission accomplished, I lay back on my bunk and waited for my rival correspondents—there were at least a half a dozen of them—to return from the field. As each did, his home office informed him that AP had the story of Seoul shelled. Most did the knee-jerk denial. Not Dick Applegate of UP, who knew me better than that. Apples went out and hunted down Colonel Dolvin, which wasn't easy as he had moved on from the spot where I found him. It was nearly midnight before Applegate found him, confirmed my story and congratulated me. "You son of a bitch," he said.

✳✳✳

It is instructive that things don't change much in the business of war corresponding. Many years on, I was working in London for NBC television and covering the Falklands War, 8,000 miles away.

The Falklands are about 300 miles off the Argentine coast, and although they have been British for centuries are also claimed by Argentina.

A military junta ruled Argentina in 1981. Possibly to provide a smoke-screen for their persistent murdering of Argentine civilians (some 20,000 "disappeared" in just a couple of years) they decided to take over the Falklands, which were guarded by one British bobby at the time.

It also became clear that Argentine leaders—generals and admirals—had calculated in their macho way that since Britain was led by a woman prime minister she would never attempt to retake the islands, and probably would collapse in tears at the mere thought, being a mere woman.

The woman in question was Margaret Thatcher.

She sent a flotilla on an 8,000-mile sea journey, mounted an invasion with forces outnumbered three-to-one, and five-to-one in aircraft. British paratroopers humped 60-pounds each of equipment over the mountains and came within range of the capital of Stanley and began shelling the Argentines inside.

Big stuff, so the top NBC correspondent in London handled the story. As soon as he finished, I got a call from New York.

"We don't want to hurt anybody's feelings, Jim," the New York editor said, "but we think that story misses the mark. Can you find a spare studio and give us one that has more zing?"

"Sure," I said, "I've got just the lead for you." And I gave them the story I wrote after shelling Seoul some 30 years before, almost word for word. It had the capital in it, and that was NEWS.

9.
SEOUL AGAIN

Shelling Seoul was one thing, recapturing it quite another. Ridgway spurred his troops to the south bank of the Han River. Seoul was on the other side, separated by at least half a mile of river. The bridge had been blown months before. Its central span drooped into the river at a crazy angle.

We could see Chinese soldiers in their brown knitted uniforms running from one dugout to another on the opposite bank.

Ridgway's next move was to outflank the Chinese force inside the capital city. His plan was to cross the river a dozen or so miles upstream to the east, drive eight or ten miles north and then turn to the west, cutting off the retreat of the Chinese forces inside the city. If they had any military sense they would evacuate the city before they were trapped inside.

A regiment of the Third Division, with which I was still embedded, was selected to make the crossing. I joined the lead battalion.

A U.S. division is a huge, self-contained community, about 15,000 strong. Its three regiments are subdivided into battalions, companies and platoons. A division had its own artillery, transport, signals, supply chain, medics, the lot. Each had a code name for telephone use. In the Third Division (code named Kaiser for its sterling work in World War I), the code names all began with *K* : King, Keystone, Kitchen (supply, of course), and my favorite, Kindness, for the Medics.

The lead battalion gathered to make the crossing in what correspondents always like to refer to as the "pre-dawn darkness." It was too dark to make out anything other than shapes. We gathered into two lines, waiting for the signal to climb into rubber boats which held about 20 men each and row across the river to the sandy beach on the other side. The sand stretched about 100 yards until it reached a clump of woods where, it was presumed, the enemy would be. They were.

A slight drizzle made the helmets of the waiting men shiny. They were holding their rifles pointed toward the ground to keep water out of the business end.

Then the signal came, and we began to shuffle forward. It was quiet.

Then I heard what sounded like a man whimpering. It was still too dark to see much, but soon I located the sound. It was coming from the man about three in front of me. He was shaking, violently, and quietly protesting that he did not want to make this landing. He was refusing to get into one of the boats.

I wondered what would happen to this poor guy. Was this cowardice in the face of the enemy? Would he be court-martialed? As in all wars, there were cases in Korea of "self-inflicted wounds," soldiers who shot themselves, usually in the foot or leg, to avoid combat. These were usually dealt with severely. What would the Army do with a man who refused to fight, just as his comrades were about to cross a river and attack an entrenched enemy less than a mile away?

I got my answer right away. Without saying a word, two men in front of me picked up the reluctant soldier in their arms, and carried him back about 20 yards and laid him gently under a tree. And quietly, without a word, they took the man's parka from his pack and spread it over him, perhaps more to hide his shaking than to shield him from the rain.

Then the two men resumed their places in line and we all continued to shuffle forward until our turns came to get in the boats and paddle across as quietly as possible.

Just as the lead boats reached the other side, our artillery opened up, hurling round after round into the woods beyond the sandy beach. Lights twinkled as each round exploded. My eyes darted from one explosion to the next. It reminded me of rapidly blinking Christmas tree lights.

The first light of day appeared as our boat reached the other side, and we jumped out and started across the beach. I looked right and left and saw soldiers crouching and running in a zig-zag fashion, rifles at the ready. I felt like a bit of a fool, crouching, moving the same way with my portable typewriter in my right hand, but it seemed like the sensible thing to do.

A few mortar rounds landed amid our soldiers and there was rifle and automatic weapons fire from the woods. I could see the tracers passing overhead. All soldiers of every Army tend to fire high in combat. I don't know why.

Bullets passing overhead make the sound of angry bees, and I always wanted to swat at them. I also always wondered: "Why is this guy shooting at me? I don't even know him." Silly, I know, but there it is.

Soldiers moved into the woods and our artillery stopped. I could hear the sound of weapons being fired in the woods and then it dwindled to just an occasional shot.

Soon soldiers began emerging from the woods herding Chinese prisoners. In one morning we eventually collected 300 Chinese soldiers, more than we had rounded up on any day of the war to date. Their comrades apparently had given up the fight and retreated north.

Within an hour the battalion commander told me his lead patrols had passed through woods into a clearing a mile north, and reported no resistance.

Years later, I was trading Korean War stories with retired General

Fred Weyand, who had been Chief of Staff of the Army. He mentioned the Third Division. "General Soule," I said. "He drank too much," said Fred. "I know, I helped put him to bed a couple of times," I said. "But he gave me one hell of a story."

I mentioned Colonel Dolvin and the shelling of Seoul. "Sounds like just the sort of thing Tom would do," said the General.

And then I told him about an interview with the battalion commander after the river crossing. "I was the battalion commander," he said. "You've changed," I said. "So have you," he said.

I was grateful for the haul of prisoners, because in those pre-cell phone days, I had to get back across the river to the south bank and find a Signal Corps telephone to send my story to AP headquarters. I got a ride back with a boatful of prisoners.

In the next days, General Ridgway exploited the landing, pushed his troops a dozen miles north, then turned left to trap the Chinese in Seoul.

And a few days after the crossing, I was standing on the south bank with a group of soldiers, looking across at Seoul. We all noticed that the dugouts on the north bank of the river seemed to be unoccupied. Could the Chinese have done the militarily wise thing and abandoned the Capital? Could Seoul be unoccupied?

There was only one way to find out. A patrol was hastily assembled, and ordered to climb into one of those rubber boats and paddle across the Han River to check on the status of the city. The battalion commander—a different one—selected a six-man patrol to make the crossing and investigate. He added a Korean interpreter. Eleven correspondents begged to be included. Somehow a British truck driver who had lost his unit got into the boat, along with a police dog named Buck. Nineteen men and a dog, with seven rifles among us.

We crossed the river without incident, and let history record that the dog was the first out of the boat on the other side. Then we began to walk. It was eerily silent.

In this city of millions, there seemed to be nobody at home. We learned later that the Chinese had ordered the entire population out of the city, and the residents were only warily making their way back, probing the situation as were we.

The six soldiers and the Korean interpreter preformed in a military manner, walking down both sides of the road, rifles at the ready. The rest of us, unarmed civilians—I had even left my portable typewriter behind—straggled along the middle of the road, hands in pockets, eyes darting right and left, searching for the sight of someone, anyone.

Then, as we neared the center of the town on our walk, humans appeared. The first were kids, jumping up and down with glee. One had a baseball bat, broken and tacked together—as we used to do in South Central L.A.—of which he seemed inordinately proud. Then some old men began to emerge from the side streets. Many wept openly. And then some women who knelt before us and clasped our knees. There was an overpowering smell of kim chee, the Korean relish which after maturing for two or three months becomes garlic squared. While we hated to hold the people we were liberating at arms' length, some of us did so in self-defense.

Someone found an abandoned handcart, and the Korean kids gave us a ride down the main street. This was the picture of "Seoul Recaptured" that appeared on the front pages the next day. Even then, the photo had to be seriously cropped to present the image of a crowd. In the picture I'm in the middle, next to the dog.

We walked to the Chosen Hotel, where the press corps had stayed when our side held the city. I walked into the kitchen, and found that the menu for New Year's Day dinner was still posted. Evidently the Chinese had not planned on a long stay if they had not even troubled to remove the evidence of the previous occupants.

I made my way to the Capitol, tucked my head inside and yelled. My voice echoed through the empty building. At the nearby university, I found a piano in the empty music room and I played Beethoven's *"Für Elise,"* a staple of every piano student in the world. It seemed the right thing to play in a schoolroom.

And then we started the long walk back through the still almost-deserted streets of the vast city, got back in our rubber boat, and dispatched the story of the recapture of Seoul. Not a shot had been fired, nor an enemy seen.

By nightfall there were thousands of American and South Korean soldiers in the city, and pushing to the north. We never lost Seoul again.

✳✳✳

I am often asked if M.A.S.H. really looked like that and if the people who worked there really acted like that. I can testify that the answer to both questions, from personal observation is yes.

Adapted from a novel by a real M.A.S.H. surgeon, the movie and the television series were shot in the foothills of Malibu, but the resemblance to the real collection of green tents pitched in the parched hills of Korea just south of the Han River was remarkable. So were the antics of the doctors and nurses.

I became very familiar with the M.A.S.H. in the first winter of the Korean War, when I had to pay twice daily visits to a Very Important Patient therein.

As the world's largest news agency, the AP has thousands of newspapers, radio stations and TV stations on its client list, called "members" because AP is a cooperative. The owners of these various outlets tend to call upon AP correspondents to show them around, take them to the sites (the Taj Mahal, *Les Folies Bergere*, the Parthenon, whatever), and play the gracious host. This holds true even in wartime, unfortunately.

In Korea, shortly after we had taken Seoul for the second time and it became clear to the American public that the war was not lost, one Very Important Visitor loomed. She was a very elderly lady who owned all the newspapers, radio and television stations in Texas that Lyndon Johnson didn't, and she decided that she wanted to come to Korea and see the front for herself, and meet some of the Texas boys who were doing the fighting.

As she was almost as frail as she was rich, many attempts were made to dissuade her. However, as her Senator was Lyndon Johnson, these were over-ruled with the caveat that the AP would assign a man to make sure nothing happened to her.

Bob Eunson, our field boss, was one of the great war correspondents of all time. He once had a portable typewriter shot out of his hand during one of the Pacific Island landings. One day, Bob called a staff meeting and read out the instructions from New York. Some unlucky sod was to take charge of this old lady, escort her to several safe places and tell her they were fighting positions, introduce her to a slew of Texans and put her back on the plane, happy and unharmed. Or else.

Eunson chose me for this ticklish assignment. "You are to meet this old lady at the airport," he ordered, "stick with her every minute, and if anything happens to her your career will go down in flames."

The next day I was at Kimpo Airport, near Seoul, waiting for our unwelcome visitor. The airfield had only recently been recaptured and its facilities were still rudimentary, to say the least. My guest arrived on a four-engine DC-4, which taxied over to the side of the runway where a couple of tents served as passenger lounges. A ladder was propped up against the side of the plane, and the door to the passenger compartment swung open.

The lady from Texas appeared in the doorway, wearing combat gear complete to paratrooper boots. Predictably, she waved her hand and shouted, "Howdy y'all."

Then she began briskly to clamber down the ladder. I was waiting at the bottom. She cleared the last rung, took her first step on Korean soil, planted her paratrooper boot on a patch of ice, slipped, fell with a terrible crash and broke her leg.

Of course, I didn't know this at the time. I merely knew she was in terrible pain, and as M.A.S.H. was just a couple of miles away, I carried her to my jeep and drove her there as quickly as I could. She was a tough old trooper, and never uttered a single moan.

The doctors at M.A.S.H. informed me she had a busted leg. They put it in a cast while I went back to the airport to rescue her bags and take them to her so she could get out of that ridiculous garb and into a dress.

In an effort to salvage my career, I went to visit my wounded charge twice a day. Flowers and candy were in short supply in the combat zone, but I managed to bring her some cans of C-Rations so she could see for herself what her Texas boys were eating. We hit it off pretty well, and she put in a good word for me at headquarters. In time the doctors agreed to let her fly to Tokyo, and thence home to Texas. The AP took no vengeance, and I was free to go back to covering the war.

10.
NORMA JEAN WITH
NOTHING TO WEAR

When the shooting stopped in Korea, the AP had a plethora of war correspondents on its hands. It shipped them here, there and everywhere. I didn't move far, to Tokyo, where my duties soon included the role of AP's Designated Golfer.

Golf had become a passion among the very important men who published and edited the Japanese newspapers, the world's largest. Three had daily circulation of over 6,000,000. They had also become the AP's most lucrative subscribers to the news service. It seemed a good idea to my bosses to keep those publishers sweet, and what better way than for them to play and beat a big *gaijin*, or foreigner. I could play in those days. I won the Monthly Cup at the most prestigious golf club just outside Tokyo but could also manage to lose, thrillingly, to an opponent of any caliber.

I performed these chores mainly at the Kawana Hotel in southern Japan, where golf could be played all year around. The Kawana Hotel was the most expensive hotel in the world and still is a world-class golf resort. It had fantastic French chefs who served Kobe beef from cattle whose daily massages with a beer solution soften them up to produce the best-tasting beef on earth. They poured the finest champagne. There were two championship golf courses, one out the front door and the other out the back.

It was February 1954. Resting up from a long hard weekend of throwing matches to our best subscribers, I was packing to make my way back to Tokyo when the phone rang. It was the big boss in the big city. "I am afraid you will have to stick it out down there for a few more days," he said, "because Joe DiMaggio and Marilyn Monroe are coming to the Kawana Hotel on their honeymoon, and I want you to cover the story." Well, somebody's got to do these dirty rotten jobs, and it wasn't my money. So I prepared to soldier on. My short game could use some work, and a few more gourmet meals wouldn't hurt.

The DiMaggios arrived. The name on Marilyn Monroe's passport, the first she ever owned, was Norma Jean DiMaggio. The newlyweds were accompanied by the O'Douls, the fine ball player and San Francisco restaurateur and his wife, June, who had been a New York show girl.

I had not met the O'Douls, nor Marilyn, before, but I knew Joe slightly from sportswriting days. Slightly was about as well as anyone knew Joe, a champion loner. I doubt if even his brothers knew him well. When I covered the Yankees in the late 1940s, DiMaggio was known to lead the league in room service because he routinely ate alone in his room. He was the absolute King of New York and Monarch of the Yankees. No one spoke, not even the manager, on the bench before a game, or in a hotel lobby waiting for the team bus, until DiMaggio broke the silence, and he was known to go a half-hour at a time without uttering a word. The Yankees were without a doubt the quietest big league team in history, as well as one of the best.

In fact, the only time I ever saw Joe in full vocal operation was the first time he tried to take Jean Simmons away from me. Jean Simmons, who is tied with Elizabeth Taylor for the most beautiful woman I have ever interviewed, was making her first trip to America. She had stopped in New York for a series of interviews and a photographic session with

Life Magazine before continuing on to Hollywood where she was under contract to Howard Hughes.

A star in British films as a teenager, she had made a considerable mark as Ophelia to Olivier's Hamlet. A confirmed Shakespeare idolater from the day I met his stuff on the stage, I was smitten by her performance and was delighted to draw the assignment to interview her for AP.

I was allotted a half-hour just before the *Life* photographer, but we were of an age and had so much fun talking we used up about two hours. We decided to stiff the photographer and go to lunch. I took her to Toots Shor, a noisy eatery where sports and entertainment celebrities mixed.

Toots had no sooner seated Jean Simmons and me at a table, when Joe DiMaggio remembered that he knew me, if only slightly, and he came over, pulled up a chair, introduced himself, and ignoring me completely, proceeded to make an outrageous pitch for Jean Simmons for a good 15 minutes. Joe could talk all right when he wanted to, and he wanted to this day.

However, his best lines were fruitless, and he eventually gave up and went back to his own table. I figured there were three reasons why Jean Simmons had shown so little interest in the attentions of the crowned King of New York. First, she was a well-brought-up girl who believed in leaving with the man she came with; second, she probably hadn't heard more than a few words because Toots Shor's was one of the loudest restaurants in town, and she was more accustomed to the more refined hush of London cafes, and third, after Joe left in defeat, she asked, "Who did you say that was?"

Joe had picked on the only beautiful woman in New York who had no idea who he was. I saw Jean some years later, and we reminisced about the lunch. "You know, he tried the same thing on me in Hollywood about five years later," she said.

When I finally delivered Jean to the studio, the photographer was furious. He had ordered an entire line of high-fashion garments in which he planned to photograph her, but the lack of time necessitated that he simply pose her in the simple street dress she was wearing. The result made the cover of *Life*, then the most important magazine in the country.

At the Kawana Hotel, I met Joe and Marilyn and the O'Douls, and was careful not to mention Jean Simmons' name. I told them I was no paparazzi, hoping to catch them in some embarrassing situation. I would not be peeping from behind every bush. I said I would appreciate a few minutes with Joe and Marilyn, possibly before dinner each evening, and they agreed. Marilyn was even on time the first night and less than an hour late the second. As it turned out I played golf with Joe and Lefty O'Doul most days. Lefty beat me, and I beat Joe.

I wrote stories for the AP about the pair, America's sweethearts at the time, and these came to the attention of Army headquarters in Tokyo. The war in Korea was over, but we still had some 400,000 men stationed there, in the dead of a Korean winter, where the winds sweep straight out of Siberia.

The Army decided to send a colonel down to the Kawana Hotel to ask Marilyn Monroe if she would consider coming to Korea for a day to entertain the troops there. The colonel asked me to introduce him and I did that evening, at the table with the DiMaggios, the O'Douls, the colonel and me.

I have read a number of silly accounts of Marilyn Monroe's trip to Korea: that she insisted on going and left a sulking DiMaggio behind, that she had made the commitment before the wedding and failed to tell Joe, that her publicists dreamed up the whole idea. What follows here is the true version.

After some small talk, the colonel turned to Marilyn and said, "Miss Monroe, we would really appreciate it if you could come to Korea for a day or two and entertain the troops. I know they would be very excited to see you. Would you come?"

And Marilyn Monroe looked straight at the colonel, and said, "Good God, no. I have never been on a stage in my life. I have no act, I know the words to only two songs, and I have nothing to wear."

Dead silence.

Finally, Joe spoke up, and said: "Honey, if the Army wants you, you really should go. Take June (O'Doul) and go see the troops."

And so she did, and I went with her. Here I was with Norma Jean DiMaggio, fresh as paint, eager to embrace life, so keen to please, so vulnerable, before fame and rough usage turned her into an addictive and suicide-prone Marilyn Monroe. We talked about growing up in Southern California, going to school there. We were of an age, similar backgrounds and both, I seem to remember, a bit surprised to find our-selves where we were, doing what we were doing, and pleased at the same time.

She did a show in Seoul, singing the only two songs she knew, wear-ing a purple sequined cocktail dress. The reaction was, to understate it, overwhelming. So she did another show, and another, ten shows alto-gether, making her way across Korea in the dead of winter. It was often 25 degrees below zero and she performed on makeshift stages, wear-ing the same dress, singing the same two songs, *"Diamonds are a Girl's Best Friend"* and *"Two Little Girls from Little Rock,"* from her 1953 film, *"Gentlemen Prefer Blondes."*

The performances are often shown on the cable channels such as A&E or The History Channel, and sometimes you will spot a fellow with horn-rimmed glasses peeping out from behind the curtain. That is me. It was often the only place I could find to stand.

It was an exhausting trip. I lost my voice shouting my stories down those dreadful Signal Corps telephone lines (they hadn't improved any since the War), and my colleague, George Sweers who was photograph-ing the events, read my stories for me, and I suspect improved them in the process. The reception at each stop was enthusiastic to the point of hysteria.

Finally, the tour was over and it was time to fly back to Japan where Joe and Lefty were waiting for their wives.

When we arrived, Marilyn turned to me and said: "You know, I never ever really felt like a movie star before."

And she turned to Joe and said, "Joe, you never heard such cheering." It was, perhaps, not the thing to say to Joe DiMaggio. "Oh yes, I have," he said.

11.
HERE AND THERE

Betty and I loved the Filipinos and I think they loved us. In nearly four years as AP Bureau Chief in Manila and numerous return trips, we gained three Filipina goddaughters who have enriched our lives immeasurably and an extended Filipino family that stretches from Manila and Singapore to New York and London.

I was the only foreigner ever elected to the Board of the National Press Club of the Philippines, a very big deal. The president of the country swears in the new officers and they had to change the oath, swearing on "my honor as a Filipino" for me. We won the election the Filipino way where electioneering is an art form. Betty and I distributed pens and pencils labeled "Becker for the Board," gave the kiddies free balloons with similar mottos, stood inside the front door every day and shook the hand of every eligible voter—citizens of the country—twice. I got a record vote total.

Betty, who had climbed Mt. Fuji when we were in Japan, toured almost every major island in the archipelago, including the beaches where MacArthur's forces landed during World War II when he made his promised return.

I covered national and local elections, a non-stop activity, and often was feted by the villagers more than the candidates were. I golfed with presidents and kings. One foursome included the visiting king of Malaya, the current president of the Philippines and the American ambassador, the brilliant Russian expert Chip Bohlen. Seeing no reason to throw the game, I managed to post the best score. I covered President Eisenhower's emotional farewell return to the country where, as he put it, he spent five years studying dramatics under Douglas MacArthur. Both General MacArthur and his father, General Arthur MacArthur who was military governor in the early years of the 20th century, were listed on the wall of the Army-Navy Club in Manila as past presidents.

Many Americans were popular, but none more so than a young man newly elected to the presidency of his own country, John F. Kennedy. His victory was so enthusiastically greeted in the Philippines that a huge party was organized at the Manila Hotel for the night of his inauguration. At 10 p.m., the Philippines president, vice president, cabinet, senate, house of representatives, judiciary and military gathered, along with all the leading American diplomatic and military leaders, to listen to JFK's inaugural address via crackling short wave radio.

Waiting for the speech, there were numerous talks and toasts. The organizers had the idea of having a Filipino introduce the American guests, and an American—me—to do the same for the Filipinos. In this capacity, I was granted a seat at the head table for dinner and the following activities. My seatmate was a stunning youngish Filipina who looked like, and it turned out was, a beauty queen of not too distant vintage, Imelda Marcos, then the young wife of a promising young congressman who had been marked out for higher things.

And what did Imelda and I talk about? Shoes? No, it never occurred to either of us. Theft of government funds on a staggering scale? No, not that, either. (I could hardly have asked, "If your husband becomes

president do you intend to steal the country blind?" although I wish I
had.) Imelda Marcos and I talked through dinner about children. She
asked if I had any. I said, alas, no. She chastised me for this omission.
"The Bible says, 'Go ye forth and multiply,' " she reminded me. I promised to do my best, and then it came time for me to go to work as a joint
emcee.

Although I saw her after that from time to time we never had another
tete-a-tete, but ironically, the mother of one of our goddaughters was
assigned the task of displaying to the foreign press Imelda's shoe collection after her husband's overthrow.

✳✳✳

The AP always grabbed at any excuse to get a correspondent into
Moscow, if only for a couple of weeks, during the bleakest days of the
Cold War when the activities of American reporters were strictly limited, both by scope and number. Hence, one winter I found myself in the
capital of the then Soviet Union, covering an international film festival.

The AP Moscow staff seized upon my presence to dispatch me to
cover as many other events as could be squeezed in. So on one particularly frosty day I was sent to stand outside a hall where Soviet and
Chinese diplomats were holding talks that were attempting to heal the
growing rift between the two Communist nations who between them
controlled nearly half the world's real estate. It was not an ideal assignment for me, as I spoke no Russian and only taxicab Chinese, but any
reporter, the AP figured, was better than no reporter, so I donned a
Russian fur hat and borrowed a heavy Russian overcoat from the office
driver, and waited for the delegates to emerge from these extremely
important discussions.

I spent a frigid hour or so, along with a handful of mostly Russian
and Chinese reporters (or spies, it was hard to tell which in those days),
when word came that the talks had broken up and the delegates were
about to depart. I elbowed my way to the front of the line and waited.
The Chinese came out first, with their chief spokesman in the lead. He
did not look pleased to see me. In fact, he paused, looked me up and

down, apparently decided I was a Russian, and spat at me. A big gob landed on my lapel. I was glad it wasn't my coat. Then he strode angrily to his car, with his delegation trailing behind.

Well, I hadn't been a foreign correspondent all these years for nothing. It was obvious to me that these Russian-Chinese talks had not gone well and that the Chinese were spitting mad at the Russians, collectively, and in my case, mistakenly.

I headed back to the AP office. At a cocktail party the night before the film festival I had met a Canadian diplomat I knew from Asian parts. I telephoned him—if the line was bugged nobody seemed to care—and told him what happened. He said he would check with a mutual friend, an Indian diplomat who was well-connected with the talks, and soon, among the three of us we had ascertained that not only had the talks gone badly, they had been broken off and the Chinese delegation was to fly home that evening. They never returned.

It made a better story than the film festival, and I told the driver to send the cleaning bill for his overcoat to the AP.

✳✳✳

Moscow was also the scene of my movie debut, which was made at considerable cost and great dismay to the producers of the film. I'm not sure which of us was the most surprised, me or the movie makers. I had arrived in Moscow late the night before, in high mid-summer and assigned a room in the Czarist-era hotel at the foot of the hill that leads to Red Square. The Soviet system had never solved the problem of making stoppers that fit the bath tubs, so visitors were told to bring their own, which I dutifully had. No one, however, had told me they also had yet to discover window shades.

In late June, in Moscow, the sun barely sets before it rises again, and at 3 a.m. I found my room flooded with bright sunlight. Jet-lagged, disoriented, I found further sleep impossible, so I put one of my stoppers in the wash basin, sloshed water on my face, and decided to take a walk.

I pulled on a T-shirt extolling the *Amazin' New York Mets* and a pair of pants and stumbled groggily out of the hotel. I started up the hill toward

Red Square, but I had not gone far before I began what I assumed was hallucinating. I began to see horses, lots of horses. And then men in strange military uniforms, something out of the Napoleonic era.

It took a minute or two before I realized that I was not dreaming. There were horses, horses everywhere, and dozens, no, hundreds of men in what I realized were French army uniforms of the 1812 period. Well, I figured, you never know what the Soviets are up to, and I plodded on, until I topped the rise.

And there, jamming Red Square was what looked like the entire Napoleonic Army. I paused in wonderment, but not for long. Dashing across the square, screaming alternately in German and French, was a very angry man. He was waving his arms furiously, and when he got closer I could see his face was distorted with rage.

And then, between the polyglot pieces of the language, and the sight of a number of enormous movie cameras mounted on platforms, all became clear.

I had blundered into the making of the film, *War and Peace*. And because there was bright sunlight at 3 a.m.—and no danger of any 20th century intruders, they mistakenly conjectured—the film-makers had decided to use the original setting. After all, the Kremlin walls had not changed since Napoleon's day, and, of course, a horse is a horse. The scene had been going swimmingly until this weirdo in a New York Mets T-shirt wandered into the midst of Napoleon's capture of Moscow.

I guess they reshot the scene, because when I saw the superb movie later, my debut had hit the cutting room floor. Pity. The Mets could have used the publicity.

12.
THE BAY OF PIGS, THE CUBAN MISSILE CRISIS AND MARILYN AGAIN

Cuba occupied a lot of my reporting time during the Kennedy administration. Hardly had JFK taken office when he was saddled with the Bay of Pigs fiasco, a landing, planned under President Eisenhower but approved by Kennedy, on the Cuban shore by several thousand Cuban refugees from Castro's Cuba. The object of the invasion was to spark an overthrow of the newly installed Communist dictatorship.

It failed miserably, and most of the invaders were captured.

After many months of negotiations, Castro agreed to release the prisoners and let them back on American soil. The world and the AP wanted to know many things about the ill-fated expedition: how the soldiers were recruited, where they were trained, what they were promised, what went wrong on the beaches of the Bay of Pigs, and how they were treated as prisoners of Castro.

The return of the prisoners was THE news story of the week, and Kennedy himself came down to Miami to greet them. It was the only time I ever got to spend any real time with him; a brilliant conversationalist who had been a newsman himself and enjoyed talking with other practitioners of the craft.

Although I speak no Spanish, the AP decided to send me to interview the prisoners and get the answers to all the burning questions. I was supplied with a young Spanish-speaking reporter who allegedly had aspirations of bigger things.

It was winter when we left New York, a cold one with snow heaped head-high around the outlying portions of the airfield that was to become known as JFK. When we arrived in Miami it was glorious summer, one of Florida's finest. We checked into a top range hotel—love those expense accounts—and I said to the young man, "Meet me in the lobby in ten minutes."

"Why?" he asked. "Because tomorrow is Sunday," I explained, "and the newspapers have early deadlines on Saturday night and I want to go to the office and write a scene-setting story."

"That's right," said this allegedly aspiring newsman. "Tomorrow is Sunday. Do we get time and a half if we work tomorrow?"

"Son," I replied—for this was my first, but alas not my last, experience with journalism's new breed—"all we have done so far is fly to Florida in the wintertime to cover the number one news story in the world." And I meant it to sting—although it probably didn't.

We picked out three prisoners and got their stories; they had been recruited by the CIA, which had assured them the Cuban people were ripe for an uprising against Castro. They trained in Honduras, then run by a pet American dictator.

They had been promised American air cover, which Kennedy had cancelled, and the invasion went wrong from the first minute when they were landed several miles from their planned destination. Some had been brutally treated in prison by a perhaps understandably miffed Castro, but after a few weeks that stopped.

I put all this into a story, and put a double byline on it, mine and the young man's who worried about overtime. It won a batch of writing prizes. (It was very long; that always influences judges of these things.) I had hoped the byline would make up for the lack of overtime pay, but I kind of doubt it.

✳✳✳

When President Kennedy reported to the nation that the Soviet Union was installing long-range missiles in Cuba which could rain nuclear destruction upon every major city in America, *crisis* seemed to be a mild description of the situation. World War III, with all that entailed including the possible destruction of the planet, loomed as a definite possibility, unless the Soviets could be persuaded—or forced— to remove the weapons.

The AP decided it needed a War Correspondent in the area and sent me to Florida where some 40,000 American soldiers were gathering. As the diplomats in Washington and Moscow wrangled, the Army practiced invading Cuba, should that become the only way to forcibly remove the missiles from Cuba. In short order, I found myself wading ashore on a sandy Florida beach, in my moccasins (I had smuggled myself aboard one of the landing craft without the Army's permission and hadn't time to equip myself properly), where we startled thousands of nesting sea birds and an occasional bemused tourist.

The practice landing was a mess, conducted as it was by a surprisingly large number of officers and men who had never seen combat— surprising because the Korean War, in which half a million men had fought, had ended less than 10 years before. I could only hope the real thing—a landing in Cuba—would be better organized, as it was obvious the AP expected me to make that landing with these guys if that should become necessary.

I remarked on the general confusion to the officer commanding our unit, Colonel Robinson. His first reaction was to demand how I knew his name. As it was spelled out in large letters on the badge over his right shirt pocket, I could not claim any feat of investigative reporting.

His reaction was, however, typical. We in the press corps were not supposed to recognize the existence of this large military force, and the members of it, in turn, were ordered not to recognize ours.

After I had explained to Colonel Robinson how I divined his identify, he softened. I introduced myself, and he said: "Please understand, Mr. Becker, that in combat this equipment would work." This equipment, both navigational and communications machines, had not only failed to keep us in contact with adjoining units, but had been deposited on a beach at least two miles from our scheduled landing place.

"No, Colonel," I was forced to explain, "believe me, in combat nothing works."

Back on station the next day, I noticed Army units setting up short range missiles in the sand. They were aimed at Cuba. In the preceding decade I had become familiar with these weapons, and I knew in which direction Cuba lay, so I reported their installation in an AP story, inasmuch as they were visible to the entire population of Key West. (I also strongly suspected that I was expected to see the missiles, and report on their installation, as part of the diplomatic arm-twisting in progress.)

The Keys were swarming with reporters from the local papers and a few from the Washington press gang who were apparently more accustomed to having their news from White House and congressional press briefings.

When my story about the missiles hit the wires, a group of them approached me and demanded to know who had told me about the missiles. I kept my secret—I had seen them myself—and reckoned that working against these people was going to be even easier than I had hoped.

The next day, the Army strung barbed wire barricades—the words "barbed wire" have always been magical words in the War Corresponding trade, and still are—all along the beaches of Key West. I reported on that, since it was obvious to any passerby, and again a delegation called on me to demand, "Who told you?"

The Bay of Pigs, the Cuban Missile Crisis and Marilyn Again

Between practice landings, the correspondents in south Florida occupied their time—as the American and Soviet leaders negotiated—with monitoring Fidel Castro's six-hour long speeches. Until that time, I had considered Olympic "speed" skating the dullest activity on earth, but Castro topped it on the boredom meter, although much may have been lost in translation.

And then, after 13 days of nerve-wracking suspense, in the words of the Secretary of State Dean Rush, "the other guy blinked." The Soviets agreed to remove all their missiles from Cuba, in exchange for the removal of U.S. missiles from its near neighbor Turkey, and a guarantee never to invade Cuba.

The Soviets also agreed to an American photo-reconnaissance plane flying over the fleet of Soviet freighters carrying the missiles out of Cuba and back to the Soviet Union, thus gathering the oracular proof for an anxious world that the Cuban Missile Crisis was over, and possible nuclear disaster had been averted.

Plans were made ready for the photo-reconnaissance flight to take off from and return to Andrews Air Force Base near Washington, with one pool reporter who would write the story on the missile-laden freighters for all newspapers and news agencies, one television crew to film the event for all, a still photographer and a radio reporter, whose output also would be distributed to every world outlet. Andrews had satellite communications equipment so the news story, TV film, photographs and radio report could be dispatched simultaneously. It was a far cry from sticking reports into the pockets of the wounded who were being evacuated from Korea, with notes to doctors or nurses asking they call the nearest AP office, as I did in the first winter of the Korean War.

As I was selected to be the pool reporter, and I was in Florida at the time, I had to hustle to Washington, where I was met at the airport by a Military Police escort, which sped me to Andrews Air Force Base. This emphasized upon me the urgency of the assignment, as did the bevy of generals and full colonels who explained to us the communications setup and how our pooled reports would be handled on our return.

We took off and it did not take long for our best laid plans to go awry. About the time we should have been spotting the Soviet freighter fleet we were instead flying in ever-increasing circles. As on the practice beach landing, we obviously were experiencing a navigational error. The pilot was unable to locate the fleet.

I had been on lots of military flights that were lost. I had once been on a bombing run over North Korea where the pilot could not seem to find North Korea. Well, it *was* dark.

Now, as we circled in an effort to locate the Soviet freighters, I urged the pilot to seek assistance. His response made it clear that, in ascending order, there were three possible sources of information he had no intention of tapping: (1) the Air Force, which had sent him on this mission and was unlikely to be pleased that the flight intended to assure a waiting world that possible war had been averted was lost; (2) the Soviet Navy, and (3) the U.S. Navy, which was the real enemy of the Air Force.

Later, when I told this story to my wife, she said: "Just like a man. Refusing to ask directions."

But then we got lucky and found the Soviet fleet, steaming in a long line away from Cuba. We began to make our photographic passes. The Soviet sailors enjoyed the attention they were getting, smiling broadly as they peeled back the tarpaulins that covered the missiles, which were strapped to each side of the freighters. We flew down the line, again and again, taking the pictures you see regularly on the cable history channels, until every one of the TV crew had enough, and it was time to head back to Andrews and dispatch our pooled story and pictures.

However, not so fast. It turned out that we had taken so much time finding the Soviet ships, and even more time photographing and re-photographing them, that we did not have enough fuel to make the return flight to Andrews Air Force Base where all those generals and colonels and state-of-the-art communications equipment were eagerly awaiting us.

The Bay of Pigs, the Cuban Missile Crisis and Marilyn Again

What to do. After hurried consultations on the radio with Andrews, it was decided that the nearest military installation with the required communications network was Puerto Rico, and we were ordered to head there, and deliver our keenly awaited reports.

None of us had ever been to Puerto Rico, but we found it easily, and landed…at the wrong airport. There are two on Puerto Rico, and we had arrived on the civilian airfield, rather than the military one where we were expected.

The pilot radioed for clearance to the correct airfield. It was denied. We did not have enough fuel to be cleared for takeoff.

There was nothing else to do but call over the fuel trucks and fill up the jet, which was duly done.

That created another problem. Who was going to pay for umpteen gallons of aviation fuel?

At this point even the pilot, who could see his career going down in flames anyway, saw the humor of the situation. He came to the back of the plane and addressed us pool reporters. "Anybody here got a credit card with a really high limit?" he asked.

Eventually, the airfield authorities were assured that the U.S. Air Force was good for the gas bill, and we made the short hop to the correct airfield, where a different but equally impressive group of generals and colonels were gathered to handle our dispatches. I drew a bird colonel who showed me where and how to send my story to the waiting world. I was sorely tempted to detail our misadventures but due to the seriousness of the situation and a rare burst of good judgment, I stuck to the straight story. The missiles were indeed on the Soviet ships and were taken away from Cuba.

I never wrote the real story. Until now.

✴✴✴

The next time I met Marilyn Monroe I was in a hotel lobby in Manhattan. After covering the Missile Crisis, I was for a brief period attached to the press corps covering President Kennedy. In this capacity I was among a group of reporters assigned to lobby-sit the President on a visit to New York, mainly to see which wing of the warring Democratic Party had the Presidential ear.

Midway through the vigil Marilyn Monroe arrived. It was no hole-in-the-corner visit. She walked in the front door, spotted some of the press corps she knew, said hello and proceeded to take the elevator to the Presidential suite. It was a very short visit; she came back down in less than 15 minutes, waved farewell and departed.

Otherwise, the President had no visitors, and at the first deadline for the *New York Times*, then a newspaper with dignity and principles, the *Times* reporter called his office. "No politician of either side came to see the President," the reporter told his editor. "In fact, his only visitor was Marilyn Monroe, and she stayed less than 15 minutes."

And, said the editor of the *New York Times*: "There's no news in that."

Which seemed like a very sensible remark at the time—and still does.

✳✳✳

Dallas, New Year's Eve, 1963. I was in the Texas city helping the AP team investigating the assassination of President Kennedy a little more than a month before. As the midnight hour approached, I was alone, except for a teletype operator, in the AP office, finishing up some story.

Lonely, far from home, in no celebratory mood even on New Year's Eve, I decided to walk the few blocks from the AP office to Dealey Plaza, the site of the assassination. It was a pleasant night, marred only by an occasional bit of rain.

When I approached Dealey Plaza, the time was 11:15 p.m. according to the big electric sign atop the Texas School Book Depository, from the windows of which the fatal shots had been fired some six weeks before. The sign alternately flashed the time and the temperature, which was 34 degrees, but it did not seem anywhere near as cold.

The Bay of Pigs, the Cuban Missile Crisis and Marilyn Again

I saw a car stop by the little park formed by the turn in the road, the turn that President Kennedy's car took, the turn that led him under the windows of the School Book Depository. Two young girls got out of the car and placed a bouquet of flowers against the base of a granite column which bears a bronze plaque, "Dealey Plaza, Birthplace of Texas."

The girls got back into their car and drove on. Another car came up, and a young man and an older one, perhaps his father, placed a basket of flowers near the bouquet.

Another car followed. And another. Soon, as the sign atop the School Book building flashed 11:55, and then 11:56, and so on, the cars were bumper to bumper, each halting briefly at the granite column to place flowers.

This was perfectly spontaneous. No one had ordered it, or arranged it, or encouraged it. The people of Dallas, hundreds of them, were spending New Year's Eve depositing flowers, and messages, near the spot where the president was gunned down.

The School Depository clock flashed 12:00. A new year. From the center of the city a few blocks away, faint sounds of a New Year's celebration drifted to us, but at the Dealey Plaza, things were quiet, just the soft swish of automobile tires on the damp streets, and the opening and closing of car doors as the occupants got out, left flowers, and drove on.

By now the bouquets and baskets numbered in the hundreds. I walked over and read some of the inscriptions. They were not eloquent. "We miss you, Mr. President," said one. It was a child's hand, and the print had smudged a bit in the rain. "In Memory of Our Beloved President." "God Bless Our President." Those were the messages from the people of Dallas, messages and flowers delivered on their own, in the evening of traditional party-going, at the dawn of a new year.

I went back to the AP office and wrote these things. The AP cleared the wire for it. It was one of my most printed stories, and later, one of my most reprinted. It was a story I had not expected, nor had Dallas. It was the real thing.

13.
GETTING MY MONEY BACK

By the time Lyndon Johnson made the first of his innumerable trips to Vietnam to check on the progress of the war, I had become a reasonably seasoned Asia hand. It had begun, of course, in China, where I had a press-box seat on the brooding civil war between Chiang and Mao, the time when our Asian policy first began to go astray.

The Korean War followed, with a side trip to follow the defeated Chiang to Taiwan (then called Formosa), and coverage of the offshore islands dispute (Quemoy and Matsu) which created extreme tension in the mid-1950s. During those nervous times, the U.S. Navy evacuated the entire population—15,000 men, women, children and their farm animals—from the Tachen Islands which were within artillery range of the Chinese mainland and could not be defended. We took the people to Taiwan and resettled them there, and I visited the now deserted island chain and wrote, "For the first time in 2,000 years of recorded history, on these tiny islands off the coast of China, no one lived, no one loved, no one laughed, no one cried, no one died."

And then, after the French had lost in Indo-China, and Vietnam had been divided into North and South, there was what became known in the U.S. Navy as the "Cardinal Spellman Sealift." The artificial dividing line between North and South Vietnam had, it turned out, stranded more than a million Catholics in the Communist North. Cardinal Spellman of New York, a major power in American politics, pushed all the right buttons and the U.S. Navy was sent to get them out. In 1954, a small fleet of Navy ships steamed into Haiphong, the capital of the North, loaded the first boat people on board, and took them to Saigon in the South. Well over a million people were moved, and I made two trips with the human cargo and wrote several stories about it, but they stirred little or no interest at home.

The first serious shooting of the Vietnam War came in Laos, and I was sent to supervise a small team of AP correspondents covering the action. Had the eventual results not been so tragically bloody, this first series of skirmishes could have taken on an almost comic opera tone. President Eisenhower had sent some 500 American soldiers—in violation of the treaty creating the two Vietnams, it must be admitted—disguised as civilian employees, to train and lead an anti-Communist army in Laos. (President Kennedy was to up the ante with uniformed advisors, and then fighting troops, but that came later.) This "civilian" subterfuge might have worked had not the military men involved insisted on retaining separate toilets for "Officers" and "Enlisted Men," which tended to give the game away. The CIA was also quite active in the area and had recruited its own battalion-sized force. Communications between the Army advised by the American "civilians" and the CIA unit were sketchy, and the press officer at the U.S. Embassy in Bangkok told me privately that when the two forces inadvertently bumped into each other, they swiftly departed in opposite directions. Some even slipped across the border into Thailand and the officer said the Embassy was being asked to help send them back. The C.I.A. also had its own airline, which flew regularly scheduled routes, carried unsuspecting passengers and actually made money.

Getting My Money Back

At the time I was in Bangkok directing AP coverage of the struggle between the government forces and revolutionaries in Laos, which along with Cambodia and Vietnam made up what had been the French colony of Indo-China. Despite the occasional comic opera-like interlude, the fighting on the central plain of Laos was sometimes intense, a precursor to the long and bloody struggle in Vietnam that was to erupt in a year or two. At the AP, we called it as we saw it, which did not make us very popular with the American Army or Intelligence, but luckily for them, people weren't paying much attention yet.

The war soon lapped over into Vietnam itself, and did not go well at the outset, and Lyndon Johnson came to see for himself and report back to President Kennedy. Johnson requested a private briefing from a couple of old Asia Hands among the Press Corps, and I was selected along with Al Ravenholt, who had been covering Asia for many years. In fact, he was married in Shanghai in 1945 and I went to his wedding.

Johnson's advance men had scheduled our briefing with Johnson at 10 a.m. on the third day of his visit. Johnson actually arrived at 10 p.m., which we were told was fairly par for the course. "He's always 12 hours late," one of his aides told us. Al and I suggested that Johnson postpone our talk—he looked totally exhausted to us—but Johnson insisted.

The three of us went into a private room, no briefing officers, no note takers, no minders. Just us, and a bottle of bourbon and three glasses on the table.

Johnson said he had asked for this meeting with the two of us, because, as he put it: "I know you newspaper guys won't give me any of that Pentagon shit." We nodded, to signal that we would not do so.

"But first," he said, "I want to talk about the man I have just met, who I think could be the Winston Churchill of Asia, the man around whom the free world could rally."

Al and I were both embarrassed. We had been in Asia for years and never spotted any such paragon, and here Lyndon Johnson had found him in just two days. It turns out Johnson was referring to Ngo Dinh Diem, the current head of the feeble South Vietnam government. He was a pint-sized Chiang-Kai-shek, a thief on a petty scale compared to the Chinese Nationalist leader who stole on a scale not to be matched until the Marcoses came to power in the Philippines.

We were aghast. "He is a mandarin and a Catholic and a crook," I pointed out. "Some day," I added spontaneously, "we are going to have to poison his soup." As it turned out, we did have to turn a blind eye to his assassination shortly after.

This of course was not what Lyndon Johnson wanted to hear. To be honest, it became clear in time that Johnson wanted to hear only what he wanted to hear.

The conversation turned to military matters. Al and I both pointed out that the French had already blown the ballgame in Vietnam, and unless we could figure out some way to explain to the Vietnamese that the last batch of big Westerners in uniforms and carrying guns were bad, while this group of Westerners in uniforms carrying guns were good, we were on a hiding to nowhere. Things were heating up. Johnson didn't want to hear that, either.

It seemed he had somehow confused Vietnam in his mind with the Alamo—if only Davy Crockett and the others had had a little help they could have won.

One of us pointed out that we had already sent 20,000 men to help, and it hadn't made much difference.

Johnson wondered how many more were needed.

Finally, I blurted out: "You could put half a million men in here and it wouldn't make any difference." It was a figure I picked off the west wall; I had no idea any one would ever send half a million men, as Johnson eventually did, as a result of the Gulf of Tonkin resolution, just 10 years after the Spellman boatlift.

That did it. LBJ exploded. He banged on the table with his huge fist—I can still see the bottle of bourbon and the three glasses bouncing around—and fairly screamed, "You no good stupid son of a bitch, that's not what my generals tell me."

I screamed right back. "I thought you didn't want to hear any of that Pentagon shit," I said.

The air was blue, and I thought I could smell a tinge of smoke from the fire that had poured out of Johnson's nostrils.

And then he switched. Completely.

He switched before our eyes into the Let's Reason Together mode. All sweetness and light. Comparing notes some years later, Al and I agreed that this personality switch had been more disturbing than the profane explosion. "And he was only Vice President," Al said. "Imagine what chance any one had to tell him the truth when he was President."

Actually, I got that chance, half a dozen years later. It came about this way.

When Johnson ran for election on his own in 1964, he was the "peace" candidate, as opposed to his rival, Senator Barry Goldwater.

Betty and I were scheduled to be in Baghdad on assignment on election day, and, worried that if Goldwater won we would get into total war in Vietnam, we arranged to cast absentee ballots for LBJ. Absentee ballots sent to places like Baghdad are sent registered mail and have to be returned the same way. It cost a buck to receive the ballots and a buck to send them back.

Johnson won, of course, and ratcheted up the war to its highest pitch. McNamara, his defense secretary, was using his slide rule to determine the damage done by X planes, flying Y missions, with Z bomb loads, neglecting to include in his calculations that you have to hit something besides trackless jungle to have any military effect. The generals were multiplying their daily body count by a factor of three or more because it looked better on paper, and a lot of brave men who were doing their duty were getting bushwhacked at an appalling rate.

Johnson passed through Honolulu on his way to install yet another hapless government in Vietnam. I was in Honolulu writing a column for the town's major newspaper, the *Honolulu Star-Bulletin*.

I addressed that day's column to the distinguished visitor, and we put it on the front page.

"Dear Mr. President," it began.

"You owe me two dollars."

"That's what it cost my wife and me to vote for you, and we want our money back."

And I went on to describe our verbal jousting at the Vietnam briefing.

After the paper came out, I looked in at the Presidential press room at the Royal Hawaiian Hotel. I met Bill Moyers, then Johnson's press secretary.

"Thanks a lot," he said.

"Oh, he read it, then?" I asked.

"He not only read it, he stood up and threw the whole damn newspaper out the window. And you can't believe the verbal explosion after he read your column."

"Oh, I think I can believe it," I told Moyers.

PART THREE–
GAMES PEOPLE PLAY

14.
GHOSTS IN THE MACHINE

Word for word, writing stories under other people's names—ghost writing—may have been more remunerative than writing under my own. It also exposed me to some of the most fascinating characters, most notably Casey Stengel, the original master of mangled English. He taught Yogi Berra everything he knew, including how to play the outfield at Yankee Stadium, where Yogi began his career, the catcher's spot being occupied at the time.

Casey was perhaps the only man ever associated with all four New York baseball teams: he played for the Yankees, Giants and the Brooklyn Dodgers, and was the first manager of the Mets. Casey also managed the Yankees to a record five consecutive World Series titles, and a record-tying total of seven in all, and it was in his capacity as manager of the Yankees that he took the young Yogi to the outfield and explained the intricacies of the stadium. Yogi listened with wonderment. Finally he said, "Gee, Mister Stengel, did you play this game?"

Recalling the incident later, Casey said, "Does the kid think I was born old?"

A couple of years after the Yankees had dispensed with Casey's managerial services on the grounds of advanced age, he was hired to manage the brand new New York Mets, who turned out to be the worst team in the history of baseball. In their first 162-game season in 1962, the Mets won 40 and lost a record 120. This left Casey in the unaccustomed position of being unoccupied during the World Series. But his name was still something to be reckoned with, so the AP engaged him to produce a daily column on the Series, and assigned me to write the column under Casey's name, and reproducing his patented phrases.

The plan was to have Casey sit beside me during the games and comment on the proceedings throughout. At the end of the game I would assemble his thoughts into an article under the byline, By Casey Stengel. Casey and I got along fine. He talked a lot and I quickly got into the rhythm of his conversation and could duplicate it with ease. Everybody was happy, especially Casey, who stayed up late to get the early edition of the morning paper—World Series games were played in the daytime then, as they should always be—to read what had been written for him.

I knew he approved, because I introduced him to my father before one game at Dodger Stadium, and he told my dear old dad, "Your son is a very good ghost." My father, a true son of toil, went, I fear, to his grave without the slightest idea of what Casey was talking about.

The chore of disentangling Casey's verbiage—he knew what he meant, and I knew what he meant, but the trick was to reshape it in words that caught the Stengel flavor but made sense to the reader—was financially rewarding.

But there came the day when I really earned the money. The scene was Dodger Stadium. I should explain that during events such as the World Series and the Super Bowl, writers—and Casey now ranked as one, if only by second hand—are lavishly and lushly entertained. The food never stops and the bars never close. This suited Casey. He loved to talk, and he liked to drink, and as long as any one, even a waiter, remained perpendicular, Casey would rattle on.

After one particularly liquid and loquacious all-night stand, Casey's seat beside me was empty when game time approached. It was still empty when the first pitch was thrown. It was not until the second inning that a hugely hung-over Stengel stumbled into the press box, slumped into the seat next to me, and promptly fell asleep.

As he resembled death in the afternoon, I decided to let him rest a bit, but by mid-game I thought it was time to alert him to the action. I nudged him. He groaned. I nudged again. He groaned. It went like that until the final putout, nary a mumbling word came from Casey's mouth. And with the last out, he came to life, rose wearily from his seat and departed, leaving me with a blank sheet of paper upon which I was expected to enscribe 1,000 well-chosen words of Stengelese.

To make matters worse, my father was at the game. He had harbored his suspicions for years that no one could be paid for attending sporting events and writing about them, and now he looked down on the oracular proof: His son, the ghost, was sitting in his seat with his head in his hands, staring out to the center field in hopes of finding inspiration there, while all about were pounding away at their writing machines. I could feel the disappointment, as I spotted my father out of the corner of my eye. Something had to be done.

I rolled in a sheet of paper, and began furiously to type: The quick brown fox jumped over the lazy dog. Over and over. Finally, I saw a beatific smile spread over the old man's face—his son was doing something—and he went away.

That put me further behind schedule, and by the time I had finished concocting 1,000 words by Casey Stengel, out of thin air, and another thousand under my own name, I was the sole remaining occupant of the press box. The press buses had long since departed for the World Series headquarters at a downtown hotel.

I had to call a cab, which was another struggle, but eventually I made it to the hospitality suite, where I found Casey Stengel standing at the bar—obviously he had downed a few medicinal boosters—telling all within earshot all about the game, which he had slept through.

"Casey, you son of a gun," I said, and I meant it to sting, "where were you when I needed you?"

Casey looked properly sheepish, and it never happened again.

✳✳✳

The most richly rewarding of all my ghost writing jobs was landed for me by my indefatigable agent, Irving Rosee, who arranged for me to ghost write the *Roller Derby News,* from cover to cover, under six fictitious names, the favorite of which was Wheels Saunders. Pure inspiration, that. Rosee's, not mine.

The Roller Derby, which is still whirling around somewhere in Southern California as "in-line rollersport," was a major fad in the early '50s, prevailing mostly among the very young and very dumb. It had acquired hours of television time, and spawned its own newspaper, which the sports editor of one of New York's major daily newspapers and I agreed to edit and write with the provision that we were never to be forced to watch the thing.

The whole dubious enterprise, *Roller Derby News* and all, was run by a charming rogue named Leo Seltzer, one of the most open-handed entrepreneurs in history. Leo kept a fat wad of hundred dollar bills in his pocket, and peeled over several whenever he was pleased, which he often was with the *Roller Derby News.* No W-2 forms for Leo.

One year Leo finagled into Madison Square Garden, no less, a skating derby World Series. It will come as no great surprise that the results were prearranged. The *Roller Derby News* went daily for the occasion. The first night about 8,000 people showed up to watch this World Series. Leo ordered the editor and me to report a 20,000 sellout crowd in the News, and we dutifully did. The second night's attendance was not as good, about 6,000 or so, but Leo wanted, and got, another headline proclaiming a 20,000 sellout. The third night was a Saturday, and for no accountable reason, a total of 12,300 people actually paid their way in to the Garden to watch this stuff. It was an all-time record for the Roller Derby, any time, any place.

Leo was ecstatic.

He dashed into the office of the *Roller Derby News,* and insisted that we announce this record attendance in the biggest type we could find. I tried to head him off.

"Leo," I explained, "we had a 20,000 sellout on Thursday and a 20,000 sellout on Friday. How can we announce a record 12,300 crowd on Saturday."

"But," Leo sputtered, "THIS IS TRUE!"

We talked him out of it.

Earlier, as I was flinging out fiction under fictitious names, I found myself with a big blank space on the back page. I had run out of names to write under, so I decided to compose a column in the style of the hog caller in charge of stimulating spurious excitement during the skating action. His name was Ken Nydel.

Under the byline, "By Ken Nydel," I concocted a column full of capital letters and exclamation points, which captured what I suppose I must call his style.

Ken came up to me the next day and asked, "Jim, did you write my column for me?" I confessed, and he said, "Thanks a lot. I really liked it." Praise will get you everywhere, of course, so I continued the Ken Nydel column in every issue.

And five or six weeks later, Nydel rushed up to me in his usual breathless manner, and said: "Jim, Jim, did you read my column this week?"

"Read it, you clown," I said, "I wrote it." He had forgotten. They often do.

✳✳✳

Then there are the unappreciative ghostees. One such was the baseball writer of the *New York Daily News,* who had a weakness for strong drink which overcame him utterly at one World Series time. He failed even to arrive for the first game.

As he was a pleasant enough chap when sober, several of us decided to ghost his Series story for him, which we dutifully did. Our hero was, alas, a no show for the second game as well, and we ghosted another piece under his name and sent it to his office.

As game three approached, so did our long absent scribe. He was still bent out of shape as he scanned the occupants of the press box through ill-focused eyes.

"Who's been writing my stuff?" he slurred. Those of us who were guilty confessed that in his absence we had thought it best to disguise his failure to attend in person by creating his stories.

"It stinks," he said, and lurched out again, leaving us to fill the void again. Happily for us, he sobered up sufficiently to perform the rest of the Series, and to be honest, I think to this day that our stuff written for him was better than his own.

✳✳✳

A ghosting job that had a sweet-sour ending came at the end of the Korean War, when both sides began to exchange prisoners of war. We had at least 200,000 of theirs, and they about 5,000 of ours. A goodly number of Chinese and Korean prisoners of war in our hands had decided not to return.

To save face, the Koreans had to find some Americans who refused to be repatriated. "They were called "non-repats." As the American and British POWs from our side began to return, we learned that a lot of them, perhaps as many as one-third, had indeed collaborated with the enemy in various ways, from ratting on their fellows to embracing communism and even confessing to atrocious but imaginary war crimes.

The AP had a photographer, Frank (Pappy) Noel, who was captured in the early days of the war and spent three years in a POW camp. When he was released, the AP flew him to Tokyo and took him to dinner with a group of friends, including my wife, Betty, who told me that in mid-meal, Pappy broke down and sobbed that it was the first meal he had eaten in three years when he could trust all the people at the table. That's how bad it was.

In the end, the other side rounded up 23 "non-repats," 22 Americans and a Brit. They were quite likely among the worst offenders.

The mother of one of the "non-repats" came to collect him from the compound where they were being kept under a guard from the Indian Army. They were being held for 60 days during which they could change their minds.

That left 22.

One day, a young lady called at the AP office in Tokyo, with a sheaf of letters in her hand. Her lover, who had deluged her with letters throughout his captivity, was one of the "non-repats," and she couldn't understand why, since he had constantly written about how much he wanted to come home to her.

The AP boss, one of the great newsmen of all time, Bob Eunson, knew he had a story. He did not exactly kidnap the young lady, but he did establish her in a suite in a hotel where opposition reporters couldn't find her, and sent for me to come back from Korea. He had a ghosting job for me.

I came to Tokyo, met the young lady, visited their love nest on the outskirts of Tokyo, became acquainted with their cat, read all his letters a couple of times, and I figured I had my man down cold. Assured by the young lady that she really wanted this boob back, I asked her to write him a letter in Japanese, which I had translated. Then I went to work, imitating her style, and composing a letter under her name. I loaded it with thinly veiled sex, dragged in the cat, described the love nest with emphasis on the bedroom and included a plea for him to stop this nonsense and come home.

It took me just three letters. The first got his attention, the second moved him to a heart-felt response, and the third brought him to the office of the Indian commander, where he requested to be a repat. (The Indian officer paid me a compliment. He had naturally read the letters, and he said he would most likely have gone to Tokyo, too, had they been addressed to him.)

The young man crossed into our lines, and arrangements were made to fly him to Tokyo to be reunited with his lady love. (I pointed out to Eunson, "I'm afraid he is really in love with me.")

The Army was good about it. They turned him over to the AP for a day, and Eunson treated the pair to a scrumptious wedding and a one-night honeymoon in a hotel suite.

The next day we turned him over to the Army, which promptly gave him 20 years in the slammer, which was, if the stories his POW mates tell are true, far less than he deserved.

And the young lady? Armed with American citizenship, she divorced the guy and married a better man, and disappeared into the body politic.

15.
FUN AND GAMES

Before, during and after the wars, crises and front page turmoil, there was always sports. There were DiMaggio and Ichiro, Ben Hogan and Nicklaus, Tiger and Michelle Wie. There was the incomparable running back Jim Brown. There were Joe Louis and Lewis Lennox, George Miken and Michael Jordan.

There was the crisp afternoon in Yankee Stadium when a haggard Babe Ruth, his camel's hair topcoat hanging loosely over his shoulders and his voice raspy from the throat cancer that was killing him, said goodbye to the crowd in the House that He Built. I wanted to strangle the little weasel from the radio network who scurried about adjusting the microphone, trying to lead the crowd in cheers like a studio audience that had to be told when to applaud, as if Babe Ruth needed to have his people cued.

And Mark McGwire, crushing one into Big Mac Country on his way to 70, and Barry Bonds stroking a majestic fly into San Francisco Bay on his way to 73, and I hope they were not both steroid-aided.

Sometimes I was there when memorable words were spoken. Sometimes I even wrote them.

✳✳✳

One mid-season morning in 1948, sportswriters were summoned to the offices of the New York Giants for an important announcement. The Giants were floundering under Mel Ott, their likeable manager and National League home run king (511, one of sport's magic numbers). They had finished last under Ottie, and looked like they were headed that way again.

The Giants were in their perennial battle with the Brooklyn Dodgers for attendance and attention. The Dodgers had won the pennant the year before, and had succumbed to the Yankees in seven of the most exciting World Series games ever played. But under their loquacious and combative manager Leo Durocher, the Dodgers were in the race again in 1948.

From batboy to general manager, the two teams hated each other. They made it to a point never to trade players, or even friendly words. For years, the Giants had ruled the New York roost, while the Dodgers were objects of fun, managing on many occasions to put two men—and once three—on base. The same base.

Durocher had changed all that. As the Giants aged and steadily slid in the standings, Durocher won the pennant in 1941, and with the arrival of first Jackie Robinson and then the marvelous catcher Roy Campanella, had turned Brooklyn into the most interesting team in all of baseball.

Jack Hand, AP's superb baseball beat writer, and I made our way to the office of the New York Giants, then on 42nd Street, expecting to hear of a managerial change, which was going to be a wrench. Mel Ott had been a Giant since a teenager, and team loyalty actually existed in those kinder gentler days before Donald Fehr became "baseball commissioner," as well as players' union chief.

Gary Schumacher, the public relations man for the Giants, wasted no time once the writers had assembled. There were at least 30 of us; New

York had nine dailies, counting the Brooklyn Eagle, and they all had two or three writers on the scene.

"Gentlemen," said Gary, "meet the new manager of the New York Giants."

And the door opened—and Ottie's successor walked through it into the room. I think we would all have been less surprised if instead of Leo Durocher a man from outer space had entered the room.

A scene straight out of a newspaper movie ensued. Writers began rushing for telephones. I was luckily in the front row, about four feet from Schumacher's desk, so I grabbed his phone and handed it to Jack, who dispatched the story to AP.

Finally the conversation dwindled to a few writers trading small talk with Durocher. Finally, somebody said, "Ain't it a shame about Ottie? He is such a nice guy."

"Yes," said Durocher, "nice guys finish last."

And there it was. The quote of the century in sports, even though the words had more or less been put in Leo's mouth. Ottie was a nice guy and he had finished last, something Durocher didn't do until many years later when he was managing the Chicago Cubs, proving that even non-nice guys can finish last, too.

✳✳✳

Long before Chris Berman, founding anchor of ESPN, famous for nicknaming players, I pinned a sobriquet on a player that not only stuck, it came to symbolize an entire team. It was the 1962 New York Mets, the expansion team that brought major league baseball back to New York after the Brooklyn Dodgers and New York Giants fled to Los Angeles and San Francisco, respectively.

The '62 Mets were truly awful. They lost a record 120 games, and two of the 162 scheduled games were not even played. Called on account of pity, I always assumed.

The Mets were also extremely amusing, even when they didn't try. They had a pitcher named Robert Miller. In mid-season they acquired another pitcher named Robert Miller. Only the Mets could have two

Robert Millers on the same pitching staff. When the acquisition of the second Robert Miller was announced, we writers asked how we were expected to tell them apart. "Use their middle initials," was the response. "What are their middle initials," we asked. The press guy looked them up. Both had the middle initial "L." Luckily, neither pitcher lasted long.

In desperate need of a catcher, the Mets acquired in mid-season a catcher named Harry Chitti, for the famous "player to be named later." At the end of the season, the Mets designated Harry Chitti as the "player to be named later," thus making him the first player ever to be traded for himself.

Under Manager Casey Stengel, who had set a record for World Series wins with the Yankees before they dropped him for getting old, the Mets were always good copy. Stengel was a famous mangler of words and manager of men. He once opined, "The secret of managing a baseball nine is to keep the ones that hate you away from the ones who ain't sure." The Mets had a beer sponsor for their broadcasts, and I once wrote, "Casey Stengel and the New York Mets were a marriage made in a brewery boardroom."

Casey had a first baseman named Marv Thorneberry. He was like the rest of the Mets, inept and unlucky. He once hit a triple and was called out for missing first base. When Stengel emerged from the dugout to argue the decision with the umpires, one said, "Don't bother, Casey. He missed second, too."

Seated one day in the press box at the ancient Polo Grounds, I watched Marv muff a pickoff throw and stroll casually after the ball, obviously forgetting that there were miles of foul ground in that oddly-shaped old ball yard. The runner sprinted to second, and spotting Thorneberry's desultory effort, carried on to third.

At that point I named the offender "Marvelous Marv Thorneberry" in my piece of the day. It was not a particularly brilliant invention. The airwaves that year were full of ads extolling the virtues of a new soap powder, called M-A-R-V, Marv, with one of those jingles you can't get out of your head.

A couple of days after I wrote my story I was mingling with the players on the field, and one informed me that Marvelous Marv wanted to brain me with a baseball bat. "Don't worry, however," one assured me. "He'll miss you."

I decided to brave it, and approached Thorneberry at his locker, which bore the homemade sign apparently crafted by his teammates: "Marvelous Marv Thorneberry."

"You've ruined my career," thundered Thorneberry. I was under the impression that he was doing that himself, but never mind. "Look at the mail I'm getting, because of your stupid article."

He opened his locker and there was a stack of letters. "Read 'em," he said, and handed me a bunch.

I did, and I couldn't see what Marv was complaining about. They were all encouraging. "You are a better ballplayer than that stupid writer," said one, and there was no arguing with that. I read through letter after letter, all condemning me, and telling him to keep his chin up.

It was obvious to me, if not to Marv, that I had done him a favor.

"How many letters have you got there?" I asked. "More than 200," he said. "And how many letters do you think Casey got this week?" I asked. Thorneberry was slow but he was not entirely stupid. He got the point. His mail outnumbered Casey's by at least ten-to-one. I had, in fact, made him semi-famous.

All he had to do was take it from there. Unfortunately he hit .179 and was soon gone.

✳✳✳

The number of people who have actually seen a perfect baseball game—27 up, 27 out, no hits, walks, errors or anything—wouldn't fill the Rose Bowl twice over. I am not one of them. I am, however, almost certainly the only one who has driven right by a perfect game in progress with a ticket to it in his pocket.

Hall of Fame pitcher Jim Bunning (later a U.S. senator) pitched the perfecto against the New York Mets at their new Shea Stadium on a summer Sunday in 1964. It was the first perfect game in the National League in more than 70 years. I had planned to be there. I had a ticket in my wallet.

But my plans came unstuck the day before, at the Congressional Country Club outside Washington, D.C. where I was covering the U.S. Open. It was the last time two rounds were played on a Saturday, and it was one of the hottest days in golf history, with all the humidity Washington is famous for in June.

Ken Venturi, who had suffered so many tragedies in majors in his golfing past, had looked like a sure winner until, almost blinded by heat exhaustion, he fluffed two little putts at the end of his third round. He had about an hour to recover, before heading out for the fourth and final round in the blazing sun.

Venturi's doctor advised him not to play. I remember talking to Arnold Palmer, who had won the Masters earlier that year, about the prospects for the final round. He gestured over to Venturi, who was slumped in a chair.

Venturi recovered, and marched out, in that splay-footed fashion of his, to work his way around the course, in that oppressive heat. I walked a few holes with Palmer who characteristically went for broke at a couple of sucker pins and shot himself out of the tournament, then switched to Venturi, who was shooting a golden round, slowly planting one foot in front of the other, walking as if in a dream.

I watched for a while, then rushed back to the press room, which was cooled down like a meat locker, to file a story, then out into the blistering sun. Back and forth, until Venturi sank the winning putt. I wrote, "Ken Venturi today slew the ghosts of his golfing past."

When the AP crew finished, we left the press room for the flight back to New York, where I was down to do the Mets game. We walked just a few feet, and I stopped by a tree and threw up for about five minutes. During my trips back and forth from the frigid press room to the steaming course I had consumed maybe 30 of whatever passed for Diet Coke back then.

I decided that I was not going to fly back to New York that night and checked into a hotel to sleep off the heat exhaustion. I asked Venturi later and he said he slept 14 hours straight.

I flew back to New York about noon the next day. In the city, I grabbed a cab. The driver had the baseball game on the radio. Jim Bunning was in the fifth inning of a perfect game when we passed Shea Stadium. I asked the driver to stop. I looked at the ticket in my hand for the game, thought about the possibility of Bunning completing the perfection, eyed my bag of dirty laundry, and decided to drive on. We reached my apartment just as Bunning made the final out. That's as close to a perfect game as I've ever been.

16.
GAMES AND NO FUN

In sports, the first 46 minutes of any regular season pro basketball game rank high on the boredom meter. So do any pro football exhibition games. Also boring are those choreographed collisions of each team's designated thug that break out on cue, usually in the second period, of almost every National Hockey League game. And dull too are the America's Cup yacht races, in which the boats are usually a mile apart and no one, including the competitors, has the vaguest idea of what is going on.

But when it comes to sheer stupefying dreariness, give me the Olympic Games, summer or winter, every time.

To begin with they are hideously expensive, and almost invariably bankrupt the host city, in addition to burdening it with half a dozen costly arenas designed for sports that will never be played again in that place. In an understandable effort to recoup some of the expense, the festivities are spread out over 17 days. That's almost two and a half weeks of endless preliminaries weeding out the thousands who have no business being there in the first place, and mind-numbing mismatches in obscure activities. These are sports like net ball, beach volleyball, archery, pistol shooting and Greco-Roman wrestling, events that, as the great sportswriter Red Smith once said, no sensible person could watch if they were contested by Playmates in your own living room, all performed before crowds of people who come disguised as empty seats.

The only reason any self-respecting sportswriter attends these things, and attempts to make literary chicken salad out of the proceedings, is to reaffirm membership in the ranks of the elite. We go because all the other top dogs go. We would all be far better off watching the things on television, although that has its drawbacks, too.

Television coverage tends to include hour after hour of fast, medium and slow motion replays of the American who finished fourth, neglecting often to tell us who won. TV directors also feel duty bound to switch instantly to a rent-a-group in the otherwise empty stands, waving the flag of the competitor in question. I have often wondered who pays for all those flags.

All this is in the Olympic spirit, helping to create animosity and long-lasting ill feeling among nations and individuals alike. It all gives chauvinism a bad name.

Believe me, I've tried to get into these things. I have jogged a lap or two on the Olympic tracks in Athens, Los Angeles, Moscow, Berlin (where the image of black sprinter Jesse Owens is thrice engraved in the stone portals to mock Hitler's evil memory), Munich, Tokyo, Mexico City (a mile high and twice as exhausting), Montreal, Atlanta, and even the original track at Olympia in Greece. I did the original Marathon, from the battlefield, site of the very moving monument to the Greek warriors who fell defeating a vastly more numerous Persian army, to the white marble stadium that held the first modern Olympics in 1896. I must confess I rode a bus most of the way. The fare was five drachmas.

I've spent countless hours watching swimming or gymnastics, where they hand out gold medals like prizes in boxes of CrackerJack, sometimes two for the same events, occasionally one for not even competing.

This is in contrast with the decathlon, where competitors put in two 12-hour days competing in 10 events and get one lonely gold for their pains.

Making it harder to take this stuff seriously is the tremendous effort required to get the inside story of a competitor who might have caught your interest. The interview room is invariably jammed by freeloaders whose only claim to journalistic employment is a letter from a relative who owns the Venue, Virginia, *Daily Blat*, or a one-lunged TV station in Nowhere, Nebraska. Also many of the Olympic stars have taken to residing in rented villas with unlisted phone numbers rather than the Olympic Village, and others depart the premises the moment their event is completed.

However, though I find it difficult to believe that adults would get involved in activities of intense interest in normal times to maybe nine people, many of my colleagues do, or at least give a good impression of doing so.

At the AP there is always a race to be first with the first gold medal of the Games. Now the results of each event are fed into the computers of each news agency, so it is normally a question of which computer can beat the others.

The first gold medal of every Olympics is awarded in 10-meter pistol shooting, conducted several miles away from press headquarters before the proverbial three men and a dog. Even the relatives of the participants don't really care.

Yet I have heard AP colleagues brag , "We had a two-minute beat on the first gold medal!" Which means that either our computer was in particularly good form, or the other computers were having a bad day. This is not the sort of thing that makes the true journalistic heart beat faster.

There is one other nagging complaint. Why do they insist on running the 1,500 meters, instead of the mile, which is the proper feature of every track and field meet in the world? After all, almost everybody knows that Roger Bannister was the first man to run a four-minute mile. Does anyone know who was the first to run a four-minute 1,500 meters?

And that's just the Summer Olympics. The winter games are even worse. Consider that almost all the Winter Olympics events are contested out of sight of the would-be spectators. Long-distance skiing, for example, allows you to catch the occasional glimpse through the trees of a suffering Swede. If you look carefully you can see at least 100 yards of the finish of all the downhill skiing events. And if you are ever in search of a misnomer, catch the best half-hour of the 10,000 meter "speed skating" race. The competitors plod around in turns and compare times at the end of the long day to find out who won.

The biathlon did provide me with a good story once. It is an event in which the contestants ski cross country for several miles, with a rifle over their shoulders, halt at a target range, and shoot at the required targets, then ski on to the finish. I posted myself once at the rifle range in time to see the lead competitor arrive, unsling his rifle, and reach in his pouch for some bullets. Alas, the poor man had lost his ammunition somewhere along the line. Leaky pocket, I guess. At any rate, he had nothing to shoot, but enterprisingly tried to bum some bullets off each rival as he came into view. Each wisely declined, shot his required rounds, and skied off. Our poor man, a Dane, was disqualified, and I made him the centerpiece of my day's story. I don't think any one wrote about the winner.

At the Winter Olympics at Innsbruck, Austria, there was the downhill skier Sami Camou from Lebanon, where they not only have cedars, they have snow, which was more than could be said for the host country. Europe had been snow starved that year, so the organizers had to buy snow elsewhere. Don't ask how one buys snow. They trucked it in and spread it on the mountain slopes for the downhill ski races. They were lavish with the snow toward the bottom of the course where the TV cameras were, but at the top, for the start, they spread out just a tiny ribbon.

Stationed at the bottom, in search of a story, I watched one skier after another dash through the finish line. When you have seen one skier finish a downhill race you have seen them all. I began to count them, to keep from falling asleep, and a good thing, too.

There were 127 entrants in the race. And 127 had started, according to the official scorer. But only 126 had finished. Who was missing? I checked and discovered it was the Lebanese, Sami Camou. Sami had apparently disappeared during his descent.

Now that was a real story. I wrote it: "Where are you, Sami Camou?" was my lead. The disappearing downhiller got international attention. The winner got a paragraph or two in his local gazette.

Having made him temporarily famous, I went in search of Sami. I found him hours later, back in the Olympic Village. He related his woeful tale.

Sami had been given the signal to start down the narrow ribbon of imported snow. He dug in his ski poles to launch him. One of the poles penetrated the thin layer of snow, hit a boulder, and threw him radically off course. Sami crashed into a tree only a few yards from the starting gate, and lay there dazed for several seconds.

So Sami had hiked down the hill the back way and had a shower and a good meal before his fellow competitors made it back.

Sami's explanation hit the headlines, too.

I scored another small Olympics coup during the making of the movie Cleopatra, during which Elizabeth Taylor and Richard Burton discovered they were made for each other.

Their love presented a problem. Elizabeth was married at the time to the singer Eddie Fisher. She initiated divorce proceedings, and the arrangements were carried out by long distance. She would issue a statement outlining her terms for a settlement, Fisher would respond with a statement of his own, and so on.

At the time, I was covering some Olympic event at a distant venue where there was a small hotel with a single telephone. I collected my story and telephoned it to AP Olympic headquarters, and when I finished, the editor came on the line and informed me that Elizabeth Taylor had just issued a new statement covering the divorce proceedings, and he was interested in getting Eddie Fisher's response.

"I understand Eddie Fisher is at the same event you are," the editor said. "Do you think you could find him and ask him for a statement? It is his turn."

I demurred. "Eddie Fisher may be here, but so are about two thousand other people." "Besides," I added, "I'm not sure I would know Eddie Fisher if he bit me on the ankle."

And with that I turned around and there was Eddie Fisher standing behind me, waiting to use the telephone.

"Wait a minute," I told the editor. "I think I may be able to help you." And I interviewed Eddie Fisher, who had to give me a story if he wanted me to get off the telephone so he could use it.

17.
OLYMPIC TERRORISM

All I expected to do at the Munich Olympics in 1972 was to write a few human interest stories. I was part of an AP team of about a dozen. We were ensconced in a big room in the Press Center, on the second floor just above the media conference room.

ABC, which had the Olympics that year, was next door. The ABC team, clad in matching puke-yellow jackets, was loudmouthed by Howard Cosell. The great sportswriter Red Smith used to cut Cosell dead, and I followed suit for several months once until I discovered he didn't know who I was, which lessened the impact of the gesture.

There were a few small apartments on the ground floor of the building. The AP had one, and Betty, also working the Olympics, and I were installed in it.

For the first couple of days of the Games all went well. The food, if you could get at it for the inevitable horde of freeloaders with no visible means of support, was fabulous. There was a relaxed spirit about the

Games, as the Germans tried to live down the memories of the notorious Hitler Olympics in Berlin in 1936, and the horrors of the Holocaust and other foul Nazi crimes.

The concentration camp at Dachau was on the outskirts of Munich. Visiting Dachau, even nearly 30 years after the war, was a shattering experience. I recalled the story told me by one of the members of the valiant Japanese American 442nd "Go for Broke" Regiment, which liberated Dachau. A battle-hardened veteran, he told of finding hundreds of living skeletons and the starved bodies of prisoners, of finding a room full of human hair shaved from the heads of the dead, of a closet crammed with eyeglasses, another with the gold fillings of extracted teeth. All this was horrifying, but, he told me, when he opened the door of a room filled from floor to ceiling with baby shoes once worn by the child victims of the Nazi horrors, he broke down and wept.

All those years later, with the human hair and the eyeglasses and the gold fillings and the baby shoes removed, although the photographs of them remained in their place, the visit to Dachau, and the events that were about to unfold, changed my view of international politics forever.

Those events began one morning with a thumping on our apartment door at 5 a.m. When I answered the door, an AP reporter told me my services were urgently required, like instantly.

I threw on some clothes and hurried to the AP newsroom, where I was informed that a gang of terrorists had broken into the rooms of the Israeli Olympic team brandishing automatic rifles and were holding the Israelis hostage.

In an effort to erase the Gestapo image, German security had been so lax as to be laughable, although things had taken a deadly serious turn now.

I sat down at the typewriter and began writing the AP story, updating it as new facts emerged. The terrorists were backed by the Palestine Liberation Organization (PLO). They were demanding the release of hundreds of their countrymen held in Israeli jails for attempting to murder Jews in Israel.

The terrorists had killed a member of the Israeli team, a wrestler, who had resisted their incursion. Twelve other Israelis were held hostage.

I could see the Israeli rooms across the courtyard, perhaps 100 yards away. From time to time, a man in a ski mask brandishing a rifle, would step outside, and then duck quickly back.

AP reporters kept feeding me information for the running story. There were eight terrorists. They had set a deadline. They demanded the prisoner release, and safe passage to a destination of their choice.

Some things we knew. We knew the Israelis did not negotiate with terrorists. We knew the German government would stall for time.

Some things we learned later. The Israeli government hurried two of its top anti-terrorists to Munich to assist and advise the Germans. They also recommended stalling the terrorists as long as possible, and then taking them to the airport with their hostages. There they recommended ambushing them. They offered to send a team of Israelis to stage the ambush. Their advice was ignored and their assistance, whether through national pride or the anti-Semitism that lies too close to the surface still in Germany and France, was refused. The Germans would handle this situation themselves.

All this we learned later.

The terrorists killed a second Israeli. There were now 11 hostages.

The standoff continued until well after dark. And then a big helicopter landed near the scene and the eight gunmen herded their 11 hostages on board. The helicopter took off, presumably for the Munich airport, where a German-speaking AP reporter was stationed.

In 20 minutes or so, the German government addressed a hastily summoned press conference in the room below our office. The conference was televised live. Jim McKay and Cosell, in their world-affairs-expert mode, introduced it.

A German government spokesman announced that the hostage

exchange had been completed peacefully, the hostages were all safe and the terrorists had been flown to a destination of their choosing. There was an AP reporter at the conference, and I could watch it on the big screen in front of me.

Nevertheless, I kept an open line to our reporter at the airport.

I began to write the story and then I heard a shout in my ear. "Jezzus Christ," said the reporter. And then a series of gunshots could be plainly heard over the telephone line. It sounded like hundreds. The reporter excitedly relayed the fact that searchlights had been beamed on the gunmen as they emerged from the helicopter. Police snipers stationed on the roofs of the airport buildings opened fire. So did policemen disguised as maintenance workers. And so did—with a vengeance—the gunmen.

All this was punctuated by a loud explosion, which turned out to be the murder of the Israelis. Five of the gunmen were killed, but one of the three survivors crawled to the helicopter, opened the door, pitched in a hand grenade and closed the door. All 11 hostages were murdered on the spot.

The German government press conference, fronted by McKay and Cosell in their mustard-colored jackets, obviously had been a cover, a ruse designed to allay the terrorists' suspicions.

I immediately poured out the story of the airport ambush as it unfolded. Only a minute or two after the story cleared the telephone rang on my desk. It was the New York headquarters.

"Our editors are saying that what you are writing cannot be true," I was told, "because they saw it on television that the hostage exchange had been completed peacefully. Howard Cosell told them so."

I vented my wrath upon the man. "I have been training for a story like this all my working life," I protested, "and you are telling me that Howard Cosell, who couldn't find his butt with both hands, knows better than I do?"

When I simmered down I finally agreed to insert in my story that the

German government had officially announced that the incident ended without bloodshed, but...

Incidentally, the great majority of the press corps in Munich believed what they had seen on television and went to bed. The *New York Times* story of the Olympic Games, revised in 1973, a year after the Munich massacre, contains this sentence:

"Everyone in Munich went to bed that night with the false news that the hostages had been set free."

Well, of course, not everyone. The *New York Times*, and ABC and who knows who else may have gone to bed that night, but the AP didn't. The AP didn't go to bed at all.

When the shooting died down at the airport, five terrorists were dead along with the 11 hostages and a German policeman.

The AP reporter on the scene revealed that three of the terrorists had been taken alive.

"That was a mistake," he said succinctly. It was a more innocent time, and in just a fleeting moment the thought flashed through my mind: "That is kind of a bloodthirsty thing to say."

It was also a very wise thing to say. Within three months, the PLO had hijacked a commercial airliner and demanded the release of the three gunmen. And the German government set them free.

When the three reached the haven of an Arab state, they even gave a press conference, exhibiting pride in their acts, and promising to kill more Jews if they got a chance.

That press conference turned out to be a big mistake for the Arabs. The Israeli government organized a hit squad that hunted those three down, and the others who had planned and supported the Munich attack. It took some eight years, but they got them all.

The day after the hostage killing, the Olympics were halted for a memorial service during which I received instruction in the German language, in which the meaning is not clear until the action verb is uttered, and it is generally placed at the end of the sentence. After the

Munich Philharmonic played the funeral march from Beethoven's *Eroica* Symphony, Chancellor Willy Brandt spoke. I was writing the story, and had an open line to another German-speaking reporter at the scene.

Brandt spoke for what seemed to me a very long time, and I asked the reporter, "What's he saying? Give me a quick quote for the story."

"I can't," was the explanation. "He hasn't come to the verb yet."

And the next day the Olympics, against the better judgment of better men, were resumed. Betty was taking dictation from the wrestling arena. The first two contestants were summoned to the ring, but refused to wrestle out of tribute to the slain Israeli Olympians.

They were disqualified, and a second pair summoned. They, too, showing considerably better sense than the authorities, refused. Common sense prevailed, and all the matches were called off for the day.

18.
SEEING WONDROUS SIGHTS

When the AP sent me to investigate the origins and history of the ancient Olympic Games, an idea sprang full blown from my balding head. The remote city of Olympia had not only housed the Games, its temple to Olympian Zeus contained the huge gold and ivory statue of Zeus, the main god of all Greece, and one of the Seven Wonders of the Ancient World. Why not visit all of the Wonders, and write about what they were and how they fared over the long centuries since the list was compiled and gained universal acceptance about the second century B.C.

The Wonder that was the statue of Zeus, created by Phidias, the master sculptor also responsible for the magnificent frieze that encircled the Parthenon in Athens (now in the British Museum, except for a couple of panels in the Louvre in Paris), had long since disappeared. Historians suggest that after the newly triumphant Christians banned the Olympic Games in 393 it was taken to the new capital of the Roman Empire, Constantinople, and was stolen and melted down in the riots that shook that city in the sixth century.

Archeologists have, however, uncovered the workshop where Phidias fashioned the huge statue, probably 50 feet in height, and have even found tiny scraps of the gold used to construct the body of Zeus. Archeologists are still unearthing fragments of the temple that housed the statue. In fact, during my visit, a German team found a portion of the temple frieze which they immediately identified as the foot of Hippodamia, the daughter of a Greek king of legend who offered her as a prize to the winner of the chariot races at the Games, and then fixed the outcome. The scene seemed a logical fit for the main temple of Olympia.

Betty joined me as I set off in pursuit of the other six Wonders. The obvious starting point was with the only Wonder that is more or less intact, the Pyramids of Egypt. (The other six have either, like the statue of Olympian Zeus, disappeared entirely, or exist in fragments in the British Museum in London, which was, naturally enough, our final stop.)

We visited the Pyramids, crawled inside to the empty burial chambers that once held the pharaohs who ordered these incredible structures, clambered to the top of the tallest one, and then took a side trip up the Nile to the magnificent Temple of Karnak, the Valley of the Kings where King Tut is buried, and Abu Simel, the temple which had been hewn out of the rock and bodily re-installed up a cliff face, after its original site had been covered by water backed up from the Aswan Dam.

These side excursions over, we took a train from Cairo to the site of the next Wonder on the list, the fabled Lighthouse of Alexandria. The light, fueled by oil and magnified by mirrors, reportedly could be seen for fifty miles at sea, warning mariners off the dangerous rocks and shoals of the southern Mediterranean shore. Ironically, those rocks have swallowed up the Lighthouse itself, which was tumbled down over several centuries by the earthquakes which plague the region, and looted for its stones for buildings on the shore which have themselves disappeared.

Betty and I stood on the edge of the sea, on the spot where the Lighthouse, all 300-plus feet of it, once stood and could see worked stones in the shallow water that had once formed part of the Lighthouse foundations. Divers were hunting for more fragments, and several pieces of columns from the Lighthouse had been salvaged from the sea and piled up on the shore.

When we had finished reflecting on the fact that Alexander the Great, who founded the city named after him, had likely stood on this same spot, as had Julius Caesar, and Cleopatra and her Antony, it was time to travel to the fourth of our Seven Wonders, the Hanging Gardens of Babylon. This meant a flight to Baghdad, which was in one of its anti-Western moods so it took some time to wrangle permission to enter.

In Baghdad we hired a taxi driver with some English to take us to Babylon, about 50 miles away across the Iraqi desert. The river which once watered Babylon has shifted its course. We found the site of the fabled city totally deserted. We three were the only humans present. Some of the imposing walls of Babylon stand, and Saddam Hussein had many rebuilt later. But the impressive Ishtar Gate with its colored tiles depicting lions and griffons, was removed more than a century ago and is now in the Pergamon Museum in Berlin.

Small signs had been posted at various spots throughout the city, indicating where the most important structures once stood. And in front of what appeared to be the vaulted foundations of the royal palace, made of clay bricks, was a sign *The Hanging Gardens of Babylon*. It was impossible on that scorching midday in totally unoccupied terrain to imagine a lofty palace with gardens, green and shady, on its roof terrace. Legend has it that a king had the gardens, soil, trees, shrubs and cooling fountains imported to satisfy his queen who had come from more verdant climes.

Our driver-interpreter reached down and pried loose a small clay brick fragment, inscribed, he said, with the name of the workers who made it, and handed it to me. "Here's a piece of the Hanging Gardens of Babylon," he said. I use it as a paperweight.

With four Wonders down and three to go, we headed to Istanbul in Turkey, which was home to two of the remaining three Wonders, and where I began to weave a tangled travel web that even the AP found daunting to unravel. As a result of the trips to the workshop of Phidias in ancient Olympia, the Pyramids, the Lighthouse of Alexandria and the Hanging Gardens of Babylon, I had submitted my largest and most complicated expense account ever, in five different currencies.

We checked into the Park Hotel in Istanbul. It was the espionage headquarters for Allied and Axis spies in World War II, and still bears an air of Old World intrigue. After a side trip to the remaining glories of Constantinople, we headed for the fifth of the Wonders on our list: The Temple of Diana at Ephesus. The temple was nearly three times as large as the Parthenon, and reportedly nearly as beautifully proportioned.

Ephesus has a storied past. Paul was hooted down there when he first brought the Christian message to the Ephesians, whose very livelihood was involved with the housing, feeding and selling of religious objects to the hordes of tourists who visited the city of marble streets to pay homage to the goddess Diana. In time, an important Christian church found root there, and there are unsubstantiated tales that many Christian figures, including the mother of Jesus, came to reside there. It is possible that the early Christians destroyed the Temple of Diana to erase the memory of the pagan cult that had grown up around it.

Even the site of the temple had disappeared below ground until a British archeologist uncovered it, as well as a few fragments of statuary which are in the British Museum. The foundations are extensive, but not, of course, very impressive in their present state. The Temple of Diana was about a mile outside the main part of Ephesus, which was a thriving city until its harbor silted up more than a millennia ago, and has been completely deserted ever since. The marble streets have since been uncovered, along with many imposing buildings, including the amphitheater where Paul stood and was shouted down. We stood on the spot where Paul preached.

G.I. Jim Becker as a Stars and Stripes *correspondent, Shanghai, 1945.*

Jim seated next to Gen. Claire Chennault and an unknown Chinese officer, covering the Shanghai war crimes trial of the Japanese who had participated in the execution of American airmen after the Doolittle raid on Japan in April 1942.

1951, in foreground wearing dark glasses, AP correspondent Jim with 3rd Division patrol that "recaptured the almost deserted city of Seoul" (and how the photo appeared on front pages). Someone found an abandoned handcart, and the Korean kids gave them a ride down the main street.

AP correspondent Jim working in an abandoned C-54 used as a correspondents' center, Suwon, Korea, 1951.

*Betty with
kitten Kukla,
Honolulu.*

Still checking out the ballgames on their Jay Buckey tour, 2002.

Then it was time to head back to our hotel in Izmir, the modern city a few miles from Ephesus. We had flown there from Istanbul, leaving the meter running, so to speak, at the Park Hotel.

Now the desk clerk at the hotel in Izmir advised us that the Sixth Wonder on our list, the Mausoleum of Halicarnassus, was actually just a half-day taxi ride from Izmir, at a town called Bodrum on the southwest coast of Turkey.

So we left a bag and a bill at the hotel in Izmir—we had another bag and bill at the Park Hotel in Istanbul—and hired a taxi to take us to Bodrum. There we received an almost royal welcome. The town mayor took us to tea, established us in his own guest room (no bill), and arranged for guides to take us up the hill behind Bodrum where the enormous mausoleum—the tomb of King Mausolus, hence the word mausoleum—once stood, visible for dozens of miles out to sea.

The next day we mounted the hill, partly by car, partly on muleback, the last yards on foot, to find the excavated foundations of the once enormous mausoleum. Earthquakes had shaken it down many centuries before, and the scattered stones had been collected to make a very large and formidable looking castle at the harbor mouth. It was a crusader castle, built by the Knights of St. John in the 13th and 14th centuries.

Scholars debate what the mausoleum looked like, but there is no doubt that it was enormous. Only the foundations have been unearthed, although British archeologists made an impressive haul of portions of the frieze and statues of horses and larger than life-size figures of a man and a woman, perhaps Mausolus himself, and his wife, Artemis, who had the tomb erected for the king after he died in the mid-fourth century B.C. The artifacts are naturally, in the British Museum.

With six Wonders down, and just one to go, we had a hotel room with a bag in Istanbul, a hotel room with a bag in Izmir, and a waiting taxi cab on its second day of hire. The seventh and last of the Ancient Wonders to see was the Colossus of Rhodes, a gigantic bronze statue of the patron of the islands of Rhodes, Helios the Sun God.

The island of Rhodes is perhaps 20 miles off the coast of Turkey, but it is Greek, and the two countries are seldom friendly, and were particularly antagonistic at the time because of the conflict over Cyprus. The mayor of Bodrum suggested that we take our taxi back to Izmir, collect our things, fly back to Istanbul, collect our other things, fly to Athens, and then fly to Rhodes from there.

"But I can see the darn island from here," I said. "Why should I drive and fly, and fly and fly again to get there?" That was a slight exaggeration. One cannot see Rhodes from Bodrum as there are several other islands in the way.

And, of course, with a Press Pass, you begin to think you are above the rules, so I decided to hire a Turkish fishing boat to take Betty and me to Rhodes to inspect the spot where the Colossus once stood and bring us back to Bodrum. The deal struck, we took off in a colorful boat with a smoky engine and a crew of three, headed for Rhodes.

Had I remembered my Homer, I would have realized that the Mediterranean weather can turn like a snake. It did. One moment we were putt-putting along in bright sunshine, with a vivid clear blue sky above, and the next, the winds were howling and the sky turned black. Waves began to curl over the sides of the little boat, and the captain decided to make a run for the nearest land, which was the island of Cos, only a third of the way to our destination. We barely made it before the storm broke in earnest.

Betty and I staggered on land and presented our passports to the authorities, who were Greek. Our Turkish fishermen were ordered to stay on the boat and ride out the storm even though all shipping in the area had been halted, including ferries.

We were escorted to a hotel which had closed for the season, and had neither heat nor hot water. Nor food. The only other occupants of the hotel were an Australian family, mother, father and two young boys. They had been sponge diving in the area and also were forced by the storm to dash for Cos. The four adults, totally unprepared for the icy winds, which turned the flowers black, shivered and shook, but the two boys climbed into their sleeping bags, zipped them up to their noses, and hopped merrily about. It was the sight of the little children that kept the rest of us going.

After a few hours, there appeared a gentleman named George, who had run a restaurant in Philadelphia for a dozen years before returning to his native island. George took us all to the town center where he arranged to buy long johns for us all, and described the bill of fare at the local restaurants. The food was fabulous.

The winds howled for three days, and with the help of George we were able to convince the authorities that in the name of mercy they must allow our Turks ashore and feed them. Then, almost as quickly as it had appeared, the storm disappeared and blue skies abounded.

And almost simultaneously, a large ferry boat pulled into the harbor of Cos. We asked whither it was bound. "Rhodes," was the reply, and we immediately boarded it.

In Rhodes, we checked into yet another a hotel, showered for about half an hour each, bought new clothes, and inspected the harbor where the once gigantic statue, the Colossus, had stood.

No one is exactly sure where it was, but the authorities have planted two small stone platforms, one on either side of the harbor mouth, where they conjecture the Colossus once was. Another victim of the earthquakes of the area, the Colossus had tumbled to the ground in the sixth and seventh centuries. An astonishing feat of bronze casting, the Colossus reputedly was at least 110 feet high, or more than two-thirds as tall as the Statue of Liberty in New York Harbor. History records that the shattered hunks of bronze were sold off to an Arab scrap metal merchant, who took weeks to cart it all away.

Mission accomplished, I telephoned the AP Chief of Bureau in Istanbul. I told him we had a hotel bill and a bag at the Park Hotel in Istanbul. Could he pay the bill and retrieve the bag?

"No problem," he said.

I said we also had a hotel room in Izmir, and a bag. Could he arrange to pay that bill, collect the bag, and bring it to Istanbul?

"We have a stringer in Izmir who can handle that," he said.

I added that there was a taxi driver in Bodrum whose meter had been running for nearly a week. Could he be located and paid off?

Slight pause. "Yes," the AP man said, "I think we can handle that. Anything else?"

"Well, yes," I admitted, "there is this Turkish fishing boat in Bodrum..."

In what could possibly rank as the eighth Wonder, the AP managed to pay the bills, collect the bags, placate the fishing boat crew, generously tip the tax driver, and deliver the luggage to Athens, from whence we flew to London to inspect the collection there of remnants of the Seven Wonders, and write the story.

My expense account for the venture is still the talk of the AP accounting office.

✳✳✳

Dozens of authors have attempted to compile lists of the Modern Seven Wonders of the World. Most are wildly different, but all include one unquestioned Wonder, the Taj Mahal in India. It is one of the most perfectly proportioned structures ever erected, and probably five times as big as people think it is before they are ushered into its presence.

It is one of the tasks of the AP Bureau Chief in India to escort important visitors to India to see the Taj Mahal, at all times and in all conditions, moonlight being the favorite, although the midday sun glinting off the white marble is almost equally impressive. Sometimes this escort assignment can be a pleasure, sometimes a bore.

That certainly was the case one blistering hot day in mid-monsoon when it came my lot to take a visiting publisher to see the Taj. I had taken an instant dislike to him and it was only deepened upon further acquaintance. He was one of those Ugly American types who wonder aloud in earshot of the natives, "Why can't those dumb brown people do things the way we do at home?"

The Taj Mahal is in the city of Agra, about 100 miles south of New Delhi, over a dreadful road, pock-marked with holes one could lose a child in, and covered, in monsoon season, with about three inches of filthy brown water.

The AP company car was a big black one, driven by a chauffeur who was so crooked they will have to screw him in the ground when he dies. I would have fired him, but it is illegal in India to sack an employee, no matter how dishonest or incapable.

Among my driver's naughty tricks was to water the gasoline, with the connivance of the service station employees. When I paid for 20 gallons of gasoline, I usually got 15 and five of water. They split the cost of the missing five gallons, I presume. As a result, the car had very little pep.

Hence, as we made our way south toward the Taj, me and the Ugly American in the back, the driver at the wheel, the car hit one of the potholes in the road hidden by the scummy water that covered it. The car stalled.

Someone had to get out and push. The Ugly American was not about to. The driver said it was not in his job description. That left me. I took off my shoes and socks, rolled up my pants legs, and waded into the filthy water and began to push. I had gotten up a pretty good head of steam when I stepped on a cow patty, and a chunk of it shot up and hit me right in the eye.

I paused. Here I was, in the middle of India, in 125-degree heat, standing behind a car containing a crook and a poltroon, in three inches of disgusting brown water, with an eye full of cow shit. Nothing could get any worse than this, I reasoned. Everything must be uphill from here.

And it has been.

I got the car started and we made it to the Taj, the sight of which again solaced me despite the company.

19.
PEOPLE WHO PLAY

The first time I saw Jack Nicklaus he was standing in ankle-deep grass brandishing a three iron. Pudgy, crew-cut, Nicklaus was playing in his third tournament since turning pro after a storied amateur career. To date, he had earned about $33.33 as a pro for a finish far down the field. (Being Nicklaus, his first professional victory would come a few weeks later, in the U.S. Open, in a playoff against the reigning king, Arnold Palmer, on Palmer's home turf.)

But now he was studying his lie in the spinach. As was his wont, Nicklaus had driven his ball into unfamiliar territory. Like the young Tiger Woods later, Nicklaus was many yards longer than his fellows, enabling him to hit shorter clubs and to launch those sky-high second shots for which he became so well-known. But he wasn't at this time. I watched as Nicklaus gouged out a divot about the size of a small house lot—strength was another of his attributes—and sent the ball soaring into the heavens from whence it nestled onto the green, giving him a putt at an eagle. No other golfer alive could have made the shot.

I was amazed. I also began to follow Nicklaus around like a pet puppy dog, forming a gallery of three with his father and his wife, Barbara, both marvelous human beings. I even baby-sat Jack Jr., but that came later. We became friends, but we did not really bond until one afternoon at a relatively minor golf tournament, where Jack and I were having lunch with a couple of the money-grubbing old lags who used to infest the pro ranks, and Nicklaus announced that he was leaving in a few days to go play in the British Open. The first prize for the British at the time was about 500 pounds, which wouldn't cover the airfare, and one of the buck chasers said to Jack: "Why go way over there, when you can play for twenty grand in the Milwaukee Open?"

At which point I butted in. "Maybe because they don't write golf history books about the people who win the Milwaukee Open," I said. Jack beamed all over me. After that we became so close that before one major tournament when a scribe asked Jack what his score was in a practice round—Jack never bothered with scores in practice—he said: "I don't know, ask Jim." He was two under.

In time, of course, Jack came to know that he was better than all the rest, and they knew it, and he knew they knew it. As the millions piled up, he never changed from the upstanding honorable man he had been when his total earnings were $33.33. He couldn't tell a lie with a gun in his back.

The superb British-American writer-broadcaster Alistair Cooke once included Jack Nicklaus among the six outstanding people he had met in his long career. My list would include Cooke himself, General George Marshall, the architect of victory in World War II and the Marshall Plan, President Kennedy, British Prime Minister Margaret Thatcher, Jackie Robinson—and Jack Nicklaus.

✳✳✳

Before Mohammed Ali became ungrateful, untruthful and a lousy fellow countryman, he was a charming young man named Cassius Clay, who came to New York with stars in his eyes and a juvenile poem on his lips. He happily acknowledged the backers back home in Louisville who had bankrolled his career, and boyishly admitted that he had patterned his act on that of a then-popular wrestler named Gorgeous George.

The depths of his unworldliness was obvious. Words clacking out of a teletype machine fascinated him. He particularly enjoyed seeing his own name spelled out, so those of us in the sports department would concoct stories about him so he could watch his name clicked out on the page. As the AP operated night and day, the office cafeteria offered breakfast at all hours.

Some of us took Cassius in for breakfast one evening when he was visiting the AP sports department, and when the bacon began crackling in the pan, he said, "That's the maggots trying to get out."

Such naïveté was easy prey, and one night when Cassius dropped in at the AP office with a companion he introduced as Malcolm X, we feared he would be quickly gobbled up, and he was. Malcolm X was a street-smart ex-con who probably had the potential to be a splendid citizen. He had the brains, but, alas, his elevator did not stop at every floor. Conversations with him can only be described as weird. It was as if he had read every other page of a book. He would make perfectly good sense for a page, and then veer off into rantings about space ships that traveled 100 million miles an hour.

However, we did not get many chances to converse with him; he was murdered in February 1965 while delivering a speech in Manhattan. And pretty soon, his friend Cassius didn't come around the AP sports department anymore.

The next time I saw him he was Mohammed Ali, and he knocked out Sonny Liston with a punch that no one, including Liston, ever saw.

✳✳✳

There was a time when I smoked, you smoked, everybody smoked. We didn't know any better. Then came the report proving that smoking kills, and many people either quit, or tried to. One of those who publicly kicked the habit was the golfer Arnold Palmer. Oddly, this happened to coincide with a slump in his golfing fortunes.

At the time I was a pack-and-a-half-a-day man, and I never wrote a word without first lighting up. If I got stuck in mid-story I would light another cigarette. Sometimes I had three burning at once.

During practice rounds for the Masters in Augusta one year, I approached Palmer with the customary cigarette dangling from my lips. Palmer snatched it right out of my mouth, tossed it on the ground and stomped on it with his golf spikes.

"When are you going to quit that stupid filthy habit," he exclaimed.

"I'd like to, but I need a cigarette to help me write," I responded.

"Tussh," said Arnold, or a word to that effect. "You don't need a crutch like that."

"Well, look at you," I said, "they say since you quit smoking you can't putt."

This was the wrong thing to say to Arnold Palmer. I am bigger than he is, but he took hold of my shirt and almost lifted me off the ground.

"Who says I can't putt," he remarked. "I'm going to win this golf tournament. And when I win, will you stop smoking?"

"Y-e-ss, Arnold," I said, and he relaxed his grip.

The bet was on. Palmer won the tournament wire to wire—his last Major victory by the way—and when he holed the final putt, I hurled my half-full pack of cigarettes in the trash can, and started to write the story.

Words did not spring easily to my fingers, a fact complicated by the idea I had to write the story entirely in verse to the tune of the Battle Hymn of the Republic ("Mine eyes have seen the glory of Arnold's Army on the march, etc."). And as I looked over the press room I thought every other desk had a pack of my brand (Salem) on it. But I persevered, and finally the story got written.

I have never smoked since, and as a bonus I was able to sell the story to three magazines over the years for rather handsome payments.

✸✸✸

Speaking of Majors, I once held the claret jug that goes to the winner of the British Open. I held it on my lap for about three hours, on the flight from New York to Akron, Ohio, for the World Series of Golf, which then pitted the winners of the four Majors in a two-day event. They were expected to bring their respective cups with them.

I checked in for the flight alongside Champagne Tony Lema, who had the British Open cup with him. He also had a bunch of other hand luggage, and the lady at the check-in counter informed him he was over the limit, and would have to divest himself of one.

"Here Jim," Lema said, "you carry the cup." I was honored.

✳✳✳

My absolute favorite quotable athlete is the quick-witted tennis player Chrissie Evert. One day a lady tennis player who had retired to raise a family brought her newest baby to the press-players lounge at Wimbledon. Several of the active players were admiring the sprout.

"Wouldn't you like to have a baby, Chris?" one asked.

"I'd rather get married first," Chrissie said. (And she did.)

During the heyday of Martina Navratilova, the inevitable question of how she would fare against men players arose. Somebody asked Chrissie, who then was ranked No. 2 among the women, where she thought Martina would be ranked among the men.

"Well, my brother beats me," Chrissie said, "and he isn't even ranked."

And when an aging tennis player decided to have his wang chopped off, paint his fingernails and enter the ladies tournament, by a quirk of fate he was matched with Chrissie.

"How do you think you will fare against her," someone asked.

"No problem," said Chrissie. "I'm used to playing against old men at my club."

At the 100th anniversary of the Wimbledon tournament, Queen Elizabeth came to center court to greet all the living winners. One little old lady who had won the doubles in 1902 came all the way from California. Others made the trip from Australia and all over the United States. All that is, but one.

The only living winner who was absent from the ceremony was Jimmy Connors, who was about 100 yards away, practicing on an outside court.

He couldn't be bothered to walk over, preferring to stiff the Queen of England.

***

The record books show that Jim Brown, the greatest running back in football history, gained more than 1,000 yards every year but one. This is no mean feat in a 12-game season and when the emphasis was on defense. In actual fact, Brown gained 1,000 in that missing season. Well, he did and he didn't.

It is instructive as to how little attention was paid to such things at the time, but in the final regular season game for the Cleveland Browns, Jim Brown carried the ball in the fourth quarter of a game he had totally dominated for an eight-yard gain. In the press box, it was duly noted that Brown had passed the 1,000 yard mark again—in fact had a total of 1,001.

But on the next play, Brown took a pitchout and was promptly tackled for a four-yard loss! Back to 997.

And with that, he was taken out of the game to rest him for the play-offs. Never mind the writers jumping up and down calling for him to get three yards. All the Browns, and Brown himself, as I learned later in the dressing room, cared about was winning the game.

When I went to ask him about it, I found him sitting on a stool while trainers dressed him, putting one arm gingerly through the sleeve of his white shirt, then the other, then tying his neck tie. He rose slowly to his feet, and they inserted his arms, one at a time, into his suit coat. This magnificent specimen who, like Ted Williams, Sandy Koufax, Oscar Robinson, Michael Jordan, Nicklaus, the Tiger Woods of 2000, played on a plane above the rest, was so battered by the long season he needed help dressing himself. He shrugged off my question. It was evident he needed no number milestone to authenticate his greatness.

***

Ben Hogan was not a man of many words. His golfing opponents used to claim that the only two words he uttered during a round was:

"You're away." Neither did he have many words for the writers who covered golf in his heyday, some of whom didn't know a drive from a divot and others who boasted that they had never set foot on a golf course to watch the play, preferring to park in front of the television screen. The fabulous writer Herbert Warren Wind had advised me when I arrived at my first tournament to pick the hole farthest from the clubhouse and go stand behind the green during an entire practice round. The players would all see you there, and respond thereafter to your questions with good will.

After winning the Open in 1948, Hogan was horribly mangled in an automobile accident. It took more than a year for doctors to patch him back together, and then for him to regain his game. And now in 1950, he was playing in the Open at the Marion Club outside Philadelphia on one of the hottest June days on record. They played the third and fourth rounds on Saturday in those days, a practice that lasted until Venturi's Open.

The searing heat had slowed play in the third round, and left the players less than an hour before they had to tee it up for the final 18 holes. As I recall, Hogan had just 45 minutes from the time he limped in from his third round, time only to change clothes and eat a ham sandwich and a glass of milk.

And that is what this great golfer was doing when I had to approach him for some quotes for my afternoon story for AP. I apologized profusely for the interruption, and prepared to take one quick quote and run, leaving Hogan to collect his thoughts for the last torturous round. After all, this was a man with a reputation for being more laconic than loquacious, and I was still an unknown rookie reporter to him. But the great man would have none of it.

He motioned me to sit down on the bench, and gave me a carefully reasoned explanation for his third round play and his plans for the fourth which he won, of course.

And when he had practically filled my notebook, this man who was faced with five more pressure-packed hours in the blazing sun, asked me: "Is that enough? Will that do?"

So much for the iceman image.

✳✳✳

Before the days of multi-million dollar memorabilia shows, many Hall of Fame ballplayers used to donate their time talking to the kids during the Little League World Series at Williamsport, PA. The year I dropped in to write about it, the two Hall of Famers in attendance were Jackie Robinson and Ted Williams, a feast for a sportswriter. Robinson, who had an IQ as big as a boxcar number, was always interesting and amusing, but the big surprise was Williams, who spent his entire career at war with the media. Williams was a master of discretion but the media wanted "mens' room rabbit ears," team members who would betray and gossip about their teammates. His playing days past, Williams opened up, telling stories about the year he hit .400 and the Triple Crowns made and just missed. (Two each.)

We also reminisced about his tour of duty as a Marine pilot in the Korean War. On one of his first missions, the North Koreans shot the landing gear off his airplane, and he had to make a 10,000-foot skidding landing on the first available emergency landing strip, which also happened to be the press headquarters. Advised of his impending arrival at the airstrip, a bunch of us followed the emergency equipment to planeside, to catch the great hitter's first words. He clambered out of his shot-up airplane, glanced at the damage, and pronounced: "_____ this _____."

As the final game of the Little League Series neared, Robinson, Williams and I were standing atop the tall tower in the midst of Little League diamonds, watching the teams practice. Williams spotted something. "Do you see what I see, Jackie?" he asked Robinson. "Yeah," said Jackie, "he can play."

I ascertained they were talking about the shortstop on a team from California, who was clearly the cream of the 12-year-old crop. I hustled down and interviewed the kid at considerable length, and then filed the notes away to produce when he made it big.

I need not have bothered. The kid was never heard of again on any level, high school, college or pro. I've forgotten his name myself.

✳✳✳

On one of several visits to the Baseball Hall of Fame in Cooperstown, N.Y., I spotted Pete Rose, the all-time hit king who was banned from the game for betting on baseball. He had set up a stand down the road and was giving autographs and promoting his constant attempt to be reinstated so his name could go on the Hall of Fame ballot. Election would, of course, be a practical certainty.

I had been among the pack of writers talking to Rose at a couple of All-Star games, so, presuming on such slight acquaintance, I approached him and introduced myself as a longtime member of the Baseball Writers Association. Its members vote on Hall of Fame candidates. I suggested to Rose that his case might be advanced if he came clean and admitted to wagering on baseball games, the cardinal sin in the sport. Pete very politely and very firmly denied ever betting on baseball, adding me to the list of writers he lied to. I suspect he saw I didn't believe him. After all, I knew writers who had seen betting slips in Pete's own handwriting.

Later in an apparent attempt to help the sales of his book, Rose came very publicly clean. He said, in fact, the biggest mistake was lying about it, which explains a lot about this magnificent baseball player with a gigantic mental and moral flaw.

Time to list the all-time best I've personally seen in action.

BASEBALL

Willie Mays. There's DiMaggio, Mantle, Aaron, Clemente, Frank Robinson, Barry Bonds and a couple ready to join them, who could take over a game. But Mays could take over a Series, even a season, in five different ways.

Best hitter—Ted Williams, with another bow to Barry Bonds. Williams gave nearly five of his best years to the service of his country in two wars, which cost him at least 200 home runs, nearly a thousand walks and maybe another .400 season. (Mays also spent nearly two years in military service.)

Best pitcher—Sandy Koufax. I was sitting on the bench watching the marvelous Bob Gibson warm up, and heard one player say: "Gibby is as fast as anybody in this league." "Fast as Koufax?" I asked. "Nah, I mean in this league, the human league," was the reply.

Koufax ranks Bob Feller, Warren Spahn, Tom Seaver, Greg Maddux (the pitcher's pitcher), Randy Johnson (saw him strike out 19), Clemens, even Gibby, who was so deliciously mean on the mound he always pitched a complete game because managers were afraid to take him out.

FOOTBALL

Jim Brown. Period.

Best quarterback—the list is long: Sid Luckman, Sammy Baugh, Otto Graham, Y.A. Tittle, Staubach, Joe Namath (best football mind), Favre, Montana, Bradshaw, Marino, but I'll still take Steve Young. All his passes hit his receivers in full stride going towards the end zone and he was the best running quarterback who ever lived.

TENNIS

Pete Sampras was refreshing, especially after McEnroe, whose temper tantrums were tantamount to cheating (he never threw one when HE was doing good), but I will take Rod Laver, the Australian left-hander.

BASKETBALL

I go back to Stanford's Hank Luisetti and George Mikan. I saw Kareem and Magic and Bird and Wilt and Michael Jordan, but the best I ever saw was Oscar Robertson. I once found him wandering around the parking lot after missing the team bus, wondering how to call a cab. "Mister Robertson," I said, "I will drive you to your hotel."

GOLF

When the Great Starter in the Sky makes up his final foursome, I think it will be Harry Vardon, Bobby Jones, Ben Hogan and Jack Nicklaus. Tiger Woods may some day edge one of them out. I saw the last three, and I cannot pick among them. I think Hogan could, in his prime, break 80 with a rake and a shovel, and Nicklaus played with persimmon heads and golf balls that tended to become elliptical. Tiger has made shots beyond the reach of any other human. I pass.

BOXING

Joe Louis. His fists struck like coiled cobras, he moved like a dancer and he was a straight shooter in the time when the mob called the shots. Jake LaMotta, the Raging Bull, once threw a fight so blatantly that some of us wrote about it—you can find my version in the Best Sports Stories anthology—and even the New York State Athletic Commission took notice. Cassius Clay, before he was Ali, clearly lost a fight against a kid named Jones and got the unanimous decision. I thought Mike Tyson was the best thing since Louis until Buster Douglas hung one on his porcelain chin. Ali would have quit against Louis, as he tried to do in the first Sonny Liston fight. In the second one Liston quit, probably on orders.

✳✳✳

Finally, double murder accusation aside, O.J. Simpson had a nice wit. A regular visitor to Hawaii for the Pro Bowl and other occasions, he often set the table on a roar in the hospitality rooms. On one such occasion, he commented on how much Honolulu, with its high rises and traffic jams, had come to resemble Los Angeles. "It's getting to the point that I can't remember which one I'm in when I'm driving around," he said. "In fact, the only difference is you can turn right on a red light in one of them, and I can't remember which city it is."

PART FOUR–
WE HAD CHOP SUEY

20.
MUSIC EVERYWHERE

In addition to instilling street smarts and color blindness, an inner city public school education in my day had the civilizing advantage of a mandatory course in music appreciation. It has probably been replaced by sensitivity training.

In the tenth grade, I was 14 and already grown to football tackle size. I remember our teacher, Mrs. Bogart, who sat us savages down and played music at us, on the piano and on records, introducing us to Beethoven and Brahms, Wagner and Verdi, and some composers then still alive, Sibelius, Richard Strauss, Stravinsky. I loved what I heard.

The next year we also had a mandatory class in art appreciation, which led to a lifetime of museum and academy visits. I could serve as a tour guide to the Metropolitan Museum in New York or the National Gallery in London, and two or three others. I remember that teacher's name too; it was Mrs. von Poderoyan.

When I expressed my pleasure to Mrs. Bogart, she suggested that I try the real thing, live and in concert. As I was a big kid, she urged me to go to the Philharmonic Hall, then the home in Los Angeles for concerts, opera and ballet, lie about my age and apply for a job as an usher, thereby assuring me a ringside seat for concerts, recitals and performances, and even getting paid in the process. I started at a buck a night, and as the wartime draft decimated the ushering ranks, I soon graduated to a more responsible and remunerative position, which I held until I got drafted in turn.

The flight from Hitler's manic tyranny and the lure of Hollywood had combined to turn Los Angeles into a cultural Mecca. The L.A. Philharmonic had in its ranks many of the world's best musicians, who played in the movie studios by day and the concert hall at night.

The orchestra was led by Otto Klemperer, soon to be succeeded by Bruno Walter, both refugees from Hitler, both among the absolute elite. Klemperer had led legendary performances of Wagner; Walter had been assistant to Gustav Mahler in Vienna in the early years of the century.

As an usher I regularly showed to their seats the composers Stravinsky and Schoenberg and the writers Thomas Mann and Bertold Brecht, and half of Hollywood, and the woman who collected more great men than any other in history, Cleopatra included, Alma Mahler.

She was married to or merged romantically with Mahler; the artist Kokoshka, who immortalized their union with his painting called The Tempest; Klimt; the architect Walter Gropius, founder of the Bauhaus and a style of building that would sweep the world; possibly Schoenberg; and the writer Franz Werfel, whose novel, Song of Bernadette, was made into a hugely popular movie in 1943. She also became the subject of a witty song by satirist Tom Lehrer in 1964.

To be frank, the woman had not worn well. She exactly resembled a dragon from one of Wagner's operas, and had the perpetual expression of someone who had just bitten into a bad oyster. But her reputation as a collector of geniuses made her the major attraction in a house full of famous people. Audience members were regularly edging up to me and asking, "Which one is Alma Mahler?"

I heard the composer-pianist Rachmaninoff in several recitals. He had hands large enough to play first base without a mitt, and incredible control of each individual finger. A tall, thin man with a serious stoop, he would sidle on stage like a human comma, but when he reached the piano and sat down at it, his back mysteriously straightened and he produced incredible sounds.

Rachmaninoff reportedly had grown to detest his popular Prelude in C sharp minor, but audiences refused to let him go until he played it. The Prelude was always the signal that the recital was over.

And there was the young Horowitz, and Rubenstein, and Heifitz, but the greatest of them all was the magnificent contralto Marian Anderson, at the absolute peak of her vocal powers, and just two years away from the most celebrated concert in our history. When the Daughters of the American Revolution refused Miss Anderson the use of the major concert hall in our nation's capital, the ironically named Constitution Hall, because she was black, Mrs. Eleanor Roosevelt, the wife of the President, arranged for her to give a concert on the steps of the Lincoln Memorial, attended by 100,000 and heard by millions over the radio.

Hers was a voice for the ages that transported its audiences on wings of song to some distant heavenly place. When the sound ceased, it took time for those of us who heard her to return to reality.

The first time I heard Marian Anderson in concert she had that effect on the entire hall. She finished her last number, and all was still. She bowed in the stately manner that was hers and moving like a monarch among mortals, she left the stage before the spell was broken and the applause began. In my innocence I turned to one of the older ushers and said, "What will she think of us? We didn't applaud."

"Don't worry, my boy," he said, "she's used to it."

After her concerts, she always sat at a table backstage and signed autographs. I used to stand in line to collect one, and then go to the back of the line to get another one. After a time, the great lady noticed my maneuvers, and would laugh with me each time I approached the table.

It was nearly 15 years before she was honored by the Metropolitan Opera as the first artist of her race to sing there, too late by her own admission, but her very appearance created a five-minute ovation. That was too late, too, but at least she was first, as was her right.

Other feasts for the eyes and ears were ushered into my life. The Ballet Russe de Monte Carlo, then the best ballet company in the west with Alicia Markova and Frederick Franklin, was stranded in the United States by the War, and spent much of their time performing in films by day and the Philharmonic at night, and so ballet entered my ken. As a would-be athlete I was immediately impressed by the skill and strength displayed, as well as the sheer beauty of it all.

And then the Opera came to town, and I was really hooked. Here was everything, music, movement, drama, scenery, costumes, all the emotions writ large. My first opera was, of course, *La Boheme*, as it is almost everybody's. Then came *Carmen* and *Faust* and the big Verdi pieces and finally Wagner, whose music aims to get inside you, get past the censor, reach those forbidden places. Many of the great Wagnerian singers of the day, including the "Great Dane", Lauritz Melchoir, were flitting in and out of Hollywood making movies and pausing to perform Wagner.

In the summer, we ushered at the Hollywood Bowl, and for a musical comedy season at the Philharmonic, which is where I discovered the meaning of the word, "star." Gertrude Lawrence came to town, with the musical *Lady in the Dark*. She could not really sing, nor could she really dance. All she had was the electricity that emanated from her to the back of the hall.

It was the same electricity that Lawrence Olivier had in spades. Maria Callas had it. So did Al Jolson. And Judy Garland on her night. The English actress Helen Mirren has it. So does Judi Dench. You can turn your back on these people, and still feel their presence.

The young Danny Kaye made his first major stage appearance in *Lady in the Dark* with an eight-minute patter song that nightly drew a five-minute ovation, which took some doing in those days before limp "standing" ovations became the mandatory norm.

As the deserved ovation for the superbly talented Kaye continued, night after night, Gertrude Lawrence stood patiently by, with a kind of wry smile on her face. And when things finally quieted down, she signaled to the orchestra which pounded out a burlesque beat so she could bump and grind her way into her big number, *Jenny Made Her Mind Up.* She shimmied up the curtain, rode a swing out over the audience and belted out the number—no ghastly mikes in those days—chorus after chorus. And when she finished, few of us could even remember the hit number that had preceded the star.

Gertrude Lawrence led me to the theater. I discovered, and about time, Shakespeare, whose entire world was the stage, and Shaw and Brecht, who was a regular concert-goer, and then the rest. I even played one of the parts in *Private Lives*, the play Noël Coward wrote for Gertrude Lawrence and himself.

In time I came to understand music and opera and ballet and the stage, and it began a parallel career for me, one that continues to this day. In the midst of wars and revolutions and tournaments and ball games, I drew assignments to cover the arts wherever I happened to be. I accompanied the Boston Symphony on its Asian tour, and still remember the hot and humid nights in a non-air-conditioned hall in Manila where the players sweated so copiously that one of the horn players lost his grip on his instrument and it slithered into the oboe section and caromed off into the flutes, creating a curious rendition of the *Eroica* symphony.

And when I was in Tokyo reporting on some very serious anti-American riots—Communist-inspired as protests against the renewal of the U.S.-Japan security agreement during some of the most frigid days of the Cold War—I was detailed to review the Kirov Ballet from what was then Leningrad, which was making its first ever appearance in the Orient. The assignment contained two revelations. One was that the Kirov, for purity of line and exquisite execution, was the best ballet company in the world at the time. The other was that the KGB minders almost outnumbered the dancers, and their surveillance was both clumsy and constant. The dancers could not eat at the hotel coffee shop without attendants.

I wrote about both. I would like to claim that my stories included my discovery of a great talent among the supporting dancers, one Rudolph Nureyev. I would like to, but I can't. It was not until some years later, after Nureyev had defected to the West, and I was interviewing him that the subject came up. Nureyev said he was so disgusted with the crude way in which his every move was monitored that he decided then and there to defect at his first opportunity. That came in Paris a year or so later.

I also drew the assignment to report on the opening of the State Theater in New York, which stands a few yards from the Metropolitan Opera House in Lincoln Center. The theater was built as a home for the New York City Ballet, under George Balanchine, with acoustics designed to deaden the sound of the dancers' shoes hitting the floor, although no one but Mr. Balanchine realized that at the time.

The Royal Shakespeare Company of England had been invited to open the new theater with a performance of *King Lear*, with Paul Schofield as the King, Diana Rigg as Cordelia and Alec McCowen as the Fool. The production had already been acclaimed in London and Stratford.

It was a colorful night. The Rockefellers, who had paid for the building, were out in force, plus the usual state and civic dignitaries, and even Lady Bird Johnson. All of us were in for a shock. When the curtain rose on the finest actors in the world, it became immediately apparent that the audience could barely hear a word. The acoustics were working exactly as designed, deadening all sound from the stage. Within half an hour, the actors realized this, and began to move forward and bellow their lines to the rafters. By intermission, they were ranged in a row across the front of the stage and acting from there.

It was several years before I found out what happened next. I was interviewing Alec McCowen, and the subject of the opening night of *King Lear* came up. He cringed.

"All actors are paranoid, as you know," McCowen said. "So we rushed backstage at intermission and demanded that someone telephone the acoustic engineer and tell him our problem. He was a laconic Dane, and we got him out of bed in Copenhagen or whatever, and somebody told him, 'We are putting on *King Lear* in your theater, and the audience can't hear a word. What should we do?'

"Long pause. Finally, a sleepy voice crept out of the telephone. 'Don't put on plays,' he said. And hung up."

Over the years, as I passed 2,000 nights at the opera, and probably an equal number in concert halls and theaters, this part-time occupation became my major journalistic activity. I contributed articles on opera, ballet and music to major publications, as well as for books, and I've probably given 500 lectures on the subjects.

As a regular reviewer I have learned a thing or two. For one, a reviewer must never diligently dig for minor flaws in an effort to demonstrate his superior sensibilities. At the same time, a reviewer must never recommend a show for which he would not spend his own money to see. It helps to check the price on the frequently free ticket in your pocket.

21.
TAKING THE AIR

The first time I saw London it was bombed flat. Even the AP couldn't find Betty and me a hotel room in town and hived us off to the suburb of Golders Green. We were put up in an Edwardian-era establishment that had somewhat escaped the Blitz, the kind of place where you put your shoes outside the bedroom door each evening and found them freshly shined the next morning.

Our first night we rolled in from an AP party, slightly stewed, the desk clerk asked if we wished to have morning tea delivered to our room and we nodded a bleary assent.

Came the dawn, and the inevitable hangover, and with them the sounds of heavy objects jangling on a tray as the hall porter approached and knocked discreetly on the door. He entered with an enormous tray laden with cups and saucers, a huge silver tea pot, an equally large silver urn that turned out to contain boiling hot water, plus silver jugs of milk and sugar, plus a clutch of silver utensils and a plate of what we learned to call biscuits.

I managed to concoct a cup of tea from all this, eyed the golden brew through bloodshot orbs, and sipped. "Voila!" The clouds lifted and the throbbing in my head instantly ceased and all was right with the world. I had discovered on my very first morning why a cup of tea is the British cure-all for everything from the Blitz to the common cold. I became addicted to the beverage on the spot, and still am, long after I have given up hangovers.

"A cuppa" was not my only discovery on this initial visit to the mother country. Without a drop of English blood in my veins, I nevertheless felt immediately at home.

Like most Americans, I had adopted Shakespeare and Jane Austen and Dickens and P.G. Wodehouse and Agatha Christie as my own, but still this sense of coming home was unexpected. I have since learned that it is extremely common among Americans with no ancestral ties to the place, including those whose background is exclusively Asian or Iberian or whatever.

I suppose it is partly the language, and the rule of law and understanding of democracy, the special relationship which cannot be completely explained nor can it be erased—and the fact that we seem to think alike and react similarly to events. This feeling was physically embodied, of course, in the greatest man of our age, Winston Churchill, who saved the western world, with his indomitable will. He had an English father and an American mother, and famously told the United States Senate that had it been the other way around, he might have made it into that body on his own.

On this first visit to the U.S., Churchill was serving out his second term as prime minister, restored to power after being voted out in the first postwar election. At the time I was too low on the pecking order at AP to rate an interview with the great man, and I never met him face-to-face.

And I also discovered, and have since had that finding reinforced, that the English are the living refutation of the old adage that no good deed goes unpunished. The French, for example, have never forgiven us for liberating their country, nor have the Germans for rebuilding theirs and defending it for 40 years. But most of the English people I've met all over the country told me they were grateful for our belated but ultimately decisive assistance in defeating Hitler, against whom they stood alone, facing long odds, for almost two years before Pearl Harbor plunged us into the conflict.

Over the years, I visited England as often as I could, sometimes making a five- or ten-thousand mile detour from my current assignment to do so. I haunted the two opera houses in London, and those later established in Scotland and Wales, the Royal Ballet, the five symphony orchestras in London, and spent weeks in Shakespeare's hometown and the London theaters. At the Old Vic, I saw Peter O'Toole's Hamlet, tall, slim, clad in clinging black and topped by blindingly blond hair. And Richard Burton's Hamlet, done all with his voice, and Olivier's Othello, Judi Dench's Lady Macbeth, Helen Mirren's Cleopatra, John Gielgud's Prospero, Anthony Hopkins, Patrick Stewart, Diana Rigg, Nicol Williamson, Ian McKellen and Derek Jacobi. And there was Alan Howard, who performed Richard II and Richard III on the same day, and followed it with Henry IV-1, Henry IV-2 and Henry V, in a morning, afternoon and evening one-day marathon. There was an unending stream of other extraordinary actors.

The arts in London wasn't all of the highest persuasion. On one trip, I "discovered" the Beatles. To no avail, as it turned out. I was walking through London's theater land en route to a performance when I heard, about two blocks away, a huge series of screams. Ever the newshound, I dashed to the source of the racket, where I found about 20,000 or maybe double that number of teenage English girls, jumping up and down and screeching repeatedly.

There was a tall British bobby standing at the edge of the crowd, looking bemused. I asked him the cause of this uproar.

"It's the Beatles, sir, "he said. That made no sense to me, so I continued on my way, but next day I appeared bright and early at the AP office in London, then just off the famous Fleet Street, home of the many British daily newspapers then. I asked about these Beatles. I thought the spelling was similar to the insect, but was quickly put straight on that point.

I was told that the Beatles were the hottest musical group in history. The cause of the uproar the previous evening had been their appearance at the annual Royal Variety Show. Furthermore, I was told, the group planned to invade the United States the following spring, and I could expect a similar reception there.

I wrote a story along the lines of "Look out America, the Beatles are coming," and dispatched it to the AP headquarters at 50 Rockefeller Plaza.

By chance, I happened to be in the New York office a few months later when the invasion of the Beatles materialized. All police leave had been cancelled and what looked like every teenaged girl in New York had collected outside the Plaza Hotel. They were launching scream after scream and leaping up and down exactly like their British cousins earlier.

I was standing next to Wes Gallagher, the big boss, watching all this on television.

"I'll bet you're glad I warned you this was coming," I said to Wes. He was surprised. "What warning," he asked. I said I had written a long story from London a few months before predicting the scene we were witnessing.

Gallagher called over the senior editor, and they launched an investigation. It turned out the man in charge on the day my story arrived in New York had never heard of the Beatles, either, and presumed, apparently, that I had lost my mind, again. So he spiked the story.

Wes Gallagher was not pleased, and I can safely say that no report of mine ever hit the spike again.

✳✳✳

When it came time to launch out in a new direction, to expand my journalistic reach, to take on radio and television full time, and to increase my emphasis on arts reporting, London in the mid-'70s was the logical place to go. I took a two-year leave of absence from print journalism, and never went back.

Of course, even in my new incarnation I could not escape wars. I was enlisted by the Westinghouse network to organize the coverage of the Yom Kippur war, in which Israel defeated in turn three invading armies, the last, to date, military attempt to extinguish the Jewish State. Having covered the same ground in earlier fighting, I gained renewed and unbounded admiration for the courage and tenacity of the Israelis in defending their homeland.

It was from London that I covered the Argentinian invasion of the British-held Falklands.

I covered the Royal Wedding of Prince Charles and Diana, which seemed a good idea at the time, a match made in heaven. One advantage radio had over television was apparent during the ceremony, when Diana messed up the order of the Prince's names, and I was able to break in and do a radio report, wondering if this was an omen, while the television droned relentlessly on.

I was also glad I was on radio and not the screen in our pre-wedding broadcast. I was hooked up from the steps of St. Paul's Cathedral to broadcasters in Los Angeles, Chicago and New York. The man in L.A. was to ask me about Diana's wedding dress (I had one of the designers at my elbow to describe it), the one in Chicago if there were many Americans in the crowd (I had two ready to talk), and New York was to request a rundown of the proceedings (I had an expert in royal weddings standing by). After I did my introduction I invited questions and the man in L.A. who was to ask about the dress instead threw me a curve. "Why does the American ambassador have such a lousy seat?" he wanted to know. On radio no one could see my reaction. Here I was outside the Cathedral without a clue where the American ambassador was sitting, let alone why. So I said, "That's a good question and I'll try to find out. Meanwhile, I have one of the designers of the wedding dress here to tell us all about it." There were no further curves.

Before the wedding, Princess Diana, as she became that day, was well known around our neighborhood; she taught pre-school in the church hall right across the street from our apartment house. Betty spotted her first, walking to work, because she was unusually tall and had that fabulous English rose complexion that runs in the royal family. It held up well once when the Princess was at the wheel of her own Jaguar, and she gently bumped into Betty amidst a mass of cars and pedestrians mingling in narrow Floral Street outside the Royal Opera House in London. Betty assured her no damage had been done and Diana's horrified expression changed and her English rose features lighted up happily.

That rose complexion. Queen Elizabeth has it, as did the late Queen Mother, and the Queen's sister Princess Margaret. I got a good close-up look at the Queen one day when I covered a knighting ceremony at Buckingham Palace. I was there because I wanted to know if the Queen says "Arise, Sir Knight," after she taps the new Sir on the shoulder with the royal sword. I was disappointed. She doesn't.

Diana of course had to give up her day job in our neighborhood after the engagement was announced. She was missed. She had brightened many lives as she loped along from the Pimlico underground station to the little school, where a tree has been planted in her memory.

However, Princess Diana was far from the most electrifying woman in England at the time. That honor belongs to Mrs. Thatcher. She sent shock waves through a room when she entered, in a classic example of how power energizes. Before her elevation to prime minister, Margaret Thatcher was a fairly frumpy housewife type with a waspish tongue, a kind of crabby caterpillar if you will. But from the day she walked into Number 10 Downing Street, the storied home of British Prime Ministers, she emerged from her cocoon as a brilliant, albeit iron-winged, butterfly, exuding authority and sexuality. This last is an almost universal observation among the press corps, even those who most disagreed with her every move.

Mrs. Thatcher met with the foreign press regularly for background sessions, although she would occasionally put a comment on the record, usually when issuing instructions to President Reagan. It did not hinder her air of authority that these meetings were usually held in the Cabinet Room of Number 10, the room in which Disraeli and Gladstone, Lloyd George and Churchill had held sway.

It was also fascinating to watch Mrs. Thatcher in the House of Commons, a lone woman amidst a pack of baying males as she ate them for lunch. And like her politics or not—and I didn't, at least at first—she changed her nation. When she took office the nationalized industries were bleeding millions of pounds a day. When the average Briton saw someone in a big black car he was likely to think how he would like to take that car away. After Margaret Thatcher, he was far more likely to feel he wanted a car just like it. And in time, he got one.

As a newsman I found radio and television a joy. At the networks where I worked, I was surrounded by amiable and capable people who seemed determined to make me look good. Cameramen, technicians, scriptwriters, even gofers, were all dedicated to your success. We were called "talent" in the trade. In print journalism, there always seemed to be about three people lusting for your job and available to take it.

Over the years, I stuck my microphone in the faces of dozens of important people, from politics and the arts. When the former governor of California, Ronald Reagan, came to town on the obligatory pilgrimage to the old country, another correspondent and I got to know him fairly well, and we each produced lengthy programs on him, which we broadcast, back-to-back, on the satellite feed to our New York headquarters.

"Nice job, fellows," said the New York editor. "Now go back and do them all over again, and this time pronounce his name correctly. It is Ray-gun, not Ree-gan."

"And you guys better get used to pronouncing it correctly because he could well be the next President of the United States."

That statement brought howls of laughter from the entire staff, most of whom indicated it was the most ridiculous thing they'd ever heard. Still, we did the pieces over and pronounced his name correctly.

I interviewed a wide range of dunces from both sides of the Atlantic, in the process of reinforcing my opinion that our youthful optimism is without foundation. In youth, we are inclined to believe that those who govern (a) must know what they are doing and (b) will think of something. By mid-career, I realized that (a) they don't and (b) they won't.

Among the half-dozen most brilliant men I ever met, the former Chancellor Helmut Schmidt, who was my most important mentor on international politics and the use of power, said most politicians want the job more than they want to do the job, and seem content to hope the ship doesn't sink on their watch.

A part-time politician I captured on camera was the immensely talented and totally weird actress Vanessa Redgrave, who stood—the British stand for office; we run—for Parliament one election as the candidate of the Workers Revolutionary Party, which is considerably to the left of Lenin. We had a pleasant talk before the cameras were turned on, and the Lady from Camelot chose to reply at considerable length in a completely incomprehensible working class accent.

"Hold it," I said, and explained that we were taping this interview for America, where she had millions of fans, and it would be appreciated if they would address them in something resembling the Queen's English, of which she was an acknowledged master. I thought she agreed to do so, although you can never be sure with her as she is very quiet and passive, odd in a revolutionary, let alone a major actress.

Anyway, we started rolling, and again she produced this "bloody, eeh, ahh, muck" accent from somewhere around the slums of Newcastle. Nothing to do but carry on and ship the finished product to New York, where I'm afraid it never aired.

I had better luck with many other artists, and immersed myself in music and dance and opera and the theater. I even collected a university degree, something I had neglected to do in my youth, with a major in the performing arts. I joined the London Wagner Society and was elected to the board. I was elected the Shakespeare Society's secretary, which is the guy who does all the work.

Taking the Air

For the Society's annual dinner one year I invited Sam Wanamaker, to speak to the Society. Sam had taken his family to England during the McCarthy witch hunts, and made his career there. He came with a harebrained scheme about rebuilding Shakespeare's Globe Theater near the spot on the South Bank where it once stood. We all thought Sam had lost his mind, but the rebuilt Globe Theater stands there today, and it is the hottest ticket in town, as it was 400 years ago.

My passion for Wagner led me to Bayreuth, the Bavarian town where Wagner lived and worked in his final years, and where the famous theater built for his works now houses the Bayreuth Wagner Festival each summer, the hottest ticket in the world. I made some of the first American network broadcasts from Bayreuth, which was revived and scrubbed of its Nazi taint by Wagner's grandsons, Wieland and Wolfgang, and which has been operated by Wolfgang since the death of his brother in 1966.

Bayreuth has been an obligatory journalistic destination ever since its first performance of Wagner's monumental Ring Cycle in 1876, at which Tchaikovsky was the critic for several musical publications. Mark Twain went to Bayreuth and wrote the famous line, "Wagner's music is better than it sounds."

In time I was received into the Bayreuth inner circle, and contributed articles to magazines and books on the productions.

In Bayreuth, Betty and I often stayed with German families in their homes near the theater, although we did spend one festival at the Gasthof Shanghai, which turned out to be owned and operated by a German-born Chinese family, no member of which had ever been within 5,000 miles of Shanghai.

One festival we were housed with the Tetzlafs. Herr Tetzlaf spoke English, but Frau Tetzlaf, a wonderful cook, had none. Betty and I decided that on our next visit to the Tetzlafs we would brush up on our German for her sake. At this stage our German was limited almost exclusively to the texts of Wagner operas, which are difficult to work into normal conversation. We went to the Goethe Institute, took lessons, bought records, practiced and eventually acquired a working knowledge of the language.

On our next visit to Bayreuth, we greeted Frau Tetzlaf in her native tongue. She was overjoyed. It seems that ever since Frau Tetzlaf had learned of our connection to Hawaii, she had thirsted to grill us about her favorite television program, *Hawaii 5-0.*

And she wanted to know all about its star, Jack Lord. I thought to myself, we spent all those months working on our German for this, but I did not disappoint Frau Tetzlaf. And as we discussed *Hawaii 5-0,* it turned out that Frau Tetzlaf actually had acquired one English phrase. It was, "Book him, Danno," the catch phrase from the television series. Trouble was, she never found a way to work it into conversation.

22.
HAWAII NEI

The AP sent me to Hawaii twice in the '50s, once as a staff member and a few years later as Chief of Bureau, so I began to get the idea that maybe I belonged there. So when in the mid-'60s, the *Honolulu Star-Bulletin*, then the dominant newspaper in the Islands, asked me to come and write a daily human interest column, I seized the opportunity. After all, the assignment completed the career path I had sketched out in the seventh grade at Foshay Junior High— sportswriter, foreign correspondent, columnist. My mother promptly sent me the yellowed clipping from the school newspaper in which I had listed my goals. "Not bad," she wrote, "and you even did it in the right order," which was more or less correct. Mothers are like that.

Hawaii is a very special place. It is, to paraphrase Mark Twain, the most beautiful place on earth, with the most blessed climate. I've been all over the world, and I can compare and contrast. Hawaii is a welcoming place. When I came to town to write a daily column for their favorite newspaper, the people embraced me almost before I had written a word. And it was wonderful to be back in the minority again.

On my first tour of duty in Hawaii, nearly half the population was of Japanese ancestry, with Hawaiians, Chinese, Koreans, Filipinos, Portuguese, and "haoles"—Caucasians—making up the balance. (In Hawaii, all Caucasians, be they Spanish, Irish, Jewish, Polish, German, Russian or whatever, are "haoles.") A quarter of the population, which has topped one million, is still of Japanese origin, although it is increasingly difficult to characterize people by race or ethnicity with the rate of mixed marriages. One of our friends is an intriguing combination of one-quarter Hawaiian, one-quarter Chinese, one-quarter Japanese and one-quarter Filipino. She married a haole to fill up the quota. A recent Miss Hawaii was described in the newspaper as Hawaiian-Chinese-Scotch-Irish-Filipino-American Indian-Japanese-Portuguese, and her mother complained the paper had left one out.

I vividly recalled a soft, summery afternoon in pre-statehood days (Hawaii became a state in 1959) when one of the innumerable Senate investigating committees had come to the Islands to check on Hawaii's fitness for statehood. The hearing was held at Iolani Palace, the former home of the Hawaiian royal family. The Hawaiian Kingdom had been overthrown in 1893 when we proceeded to steal the place, over the expressed objections of nearly 100 percent of the Hawaiians. The Legislature of the then Territory of Hawaii held its sessions at Iolani Palace. One visiting Southern senator had a question for the then-Governor of Hawaii Samuel Wilder King, himself an interesting blend of Hawaiian and descendants of the New England missionaries who had engineered the overthrow. It was a question that was prominent in the thinking of people on the Mainland.

"Governor," the senator drawled, "how do you handle your minority problems out here?"

"Senator," said Governor King, "in Hawaii we are all in the minority." True then, true now. Wonderful state of affairs.

During those early tours, one of Governor King's predecessors had enlisted me for the only unwelcome assignment I ever had in Hawaii: witness to an execution. Capital punishment was still legal in the territory, and it was customary in Hawaii, as elsewhere, to appoint official witnesses from the ranks of the press, usually from the staffs of the wire services. This was perhaps on the grounds that they were likely to be moving on and not settle down to become part of a community so closely knit that it is dangerous to say anything bad ("talk stink," in the local jargon) about anyone as he is almost certain to be somebody's cousin.

At first, I accepted the assignment of witnessing the hanging of two men who were undoubtedly guilty of robbery, rape and murder. After all, a story is a story, duty is duty, and I had seen men die before. Once I was talking to a soldier in Korea who walked around the corner and was shot dead 15 seconds later.

But as the hanging hour approached, my opinion on capital punishment, never enthusiastically affirmative, began to shift. So did that of my fellow witness, a UP reporter. The night before the hanging, which was scheduled for 8 a.m., the two of us gathered to ponder our options. At midnight we telephoned the Governor, and revealed to him that we were having second thoughts and perhaps he could call the whole thing off. He sympathized with us, but made no promises.

We repeated the call several more times. We couldn't sleep, and neither, it seemed, could the Governor. Came the dawn, a hungover one for both official witnesses, and we made our reluctant way to the prison. At 7:30 we were ushered, along with prison officials, into a room with a dozen chairs and a glass window opening onto a noose hanging from the crossbar of the gallows. We all sat, silently. At five minutes to eight, a side door in the room opposite the plate glass window opened. "Here we go," I thought. "The condemned men are about to enter." It was not a sight I wanted to see.

But it turned out to be a prison official, come to announce that the Governor had reprieved the pair, and commuted their sentences to life in prison. For one of them that wasn't long; he was killed in a prison knife fight a couple of years later. The other was paroled after 25 years, and one day he was pointed out to me at a shopping mall. "That's the man you almost saw executed," I was told. I resisted the temptation to go up and introduce myself.

When I started my stint as a columnist, capital punishment had been abandoned, Statehood had been granted despite the fact that the entire population was in the minority, and there had been a political revolution.

For decades after the 1893 overthrow of the Hawaiian Monarchy, an oligarchy, made up of the descendants of the missionaries and merchants who began arriving in Hawaii after 1820, had ruled every aspect of political and economic life. Their firms, known as the Big Five, with interlocking boards of directors, owned the plantations that grew sugar and pineapple, the ships that took those products to the Mainland, the stores that sold the consumer goods that the ships brought on their return journeys. Competition was not welcome. Even Sears had to sneak into town. An Oriental Exclusion Act was in full force. Only haoles could join the most important clubs and own land in the most desirable places. The best private schools had strict quotas for non-haoles.

The author James Michener, after he scored his major success with his novel, *Hawaii*, was refused permission to buy the beachfront house he wanted because his wife was an American of Japanese ancestry born and reared in Chicago. He left the Islands in disgust and despair.

There was, of course, one thing to be said of the plantation system. Those at the top at least were "of the land," sixth and seventh generations, and the money they made stayed here. And the mansions they built were tasteful and discreet.

Today, sugar is dead and pineapple canning, too, and almost every enterprise, from the tourist hotels to the public utilities and the retail outlets, is owned and operated from New Jersey or Australia or Osaka, and the strands are littered with gaudy and obtrusive palaces for pop stars and pizza magnates. And today, Sears competes with Wal-Mart.

There has been a seismic political shift, too. The plantation aristocracy had chosen the Republican Party as their instrument of government, and frequently held margins of 14-1 in the Territorial Senate and 23-2 in the House. Now the climate was changing about 180 degrees. Sons of plantation workers had come back from the war like the much-decorated 442nd Regimental Combat Team made up of soldiers of Japanese ancestry, mostly volunteers from Hawaii. They provided the driving force, using the GI Bill of Rights to go to law school, and forming the Democratic Party. Previously Democratic candidates had been forbidden even to speak on plantation grounds. Now they joined forces with the unions, which organized the ports, and the sugar and pineapple workers, to take over political power.

There was one fascinating period when the transition was not yet complete, and both parties in the Territorial Legislature were led by Japanese Americans. It was during this period that Indonesian dictator Sukarno visited Hawaii, and Governor King assigned me to be his escort. As we watched the Legislature in action, Sukarno noted the large number of Asian faces on the floor, and nudged me. "Which party are the Orientals," he asked. "Both of them," I replied, truthfully.

A new Hawaii welcomed me to my career as a daily columnist. I was determined to repay their kindnesses. For one thing, I wanted to write about the ordinary people of this lovely place, instead of the privileged few. My raw material would be people who normally would never see their names in the paper. I was also guided by the advice of a wise man named Webley Edwards, for decades the host of a radio and then television program known as "Hawaii Calls," and the most trusted voice in the Islands. It was Webley Edwards who was called on to assure the people that the Japanese attack on Pearl Harbor was not a drill – there'd been dozens in the preceding months—but the "real McCoy."

Webley called me aside in my first days and gave me the best piece of advice I ever got. "Remember, always," Webley said, "that half of the people who read you go to church regularly." He did not mean religious extremists or Holy Rollers. He meant, expressed in easily understandable verbal shorthand, regular people who dressed nicely, and even put on shoes (people in Hawaii like to go barefoot inside and outside the house) and go to church, with no fuss or furors. They are the often forgotten many.

So I wrote about regular people, doing the things they do, at work and at play. I liked them and they liked me and I knew I had made it when a few months into the columning craft, I found myself in a remote part of Oahu with no money or credit card, and the people in a little variety store cashed a check for me. That's recognition.

I was deluged with requests to write about this or that, and one day I got a call from the principal of Radford High School, which is on the edge of Pearl Harbor and has a student body of military kids and "locals," which is what we call people who have intermarried so much as to be unclassifiable. The military kids and the local kids did not always get along. There are horses for courses and people for places, and Hawaii is not for everyone, particularly those not born here. Many come and blend in—we speak a little more softly and act a little more kindly than others—but some have been in Hawaii 30 years and still talk of Texas or Tennessee as home.

The principal wanted me to come to Radford and write something positive about the school, and I agreed. When I arrived, I asked if there were any activities that could form the basis of a column. "We're rehearsing the school play," the principal said, and directed me to the auditorium.

I stuck my head in the side door of the auditorium. By now it was a fairly well-known head, large versions of it having been plastered on the sides of *Star-Bulletin* delivery trucks for months. I heard a squeal from the stage, where the student actors were conducting a rehearsal. "That's Jim Becker," screamed one young lady, and she dashed the length of the auditorium and jumped into my arms. It was either catch her or let her plop on the auditorium floor. I caught her, and put her down, and I said, "Okay, little girl, you win. I'll put your name in the paper. What is it?" "Bette Midler," she replied.

Bette was of course the star of the school play, the president of the senior class, and the officer of almost every other organization in the school. She went on to the University of Hawaii, where she studied drama and played Shakespeare, Oscar Wilde, Noel Coward. She even did a little singing.

When they made the movie, *Hawaii,* Bette landed the part of a missionary wife on the long voyage here from New England, and made enough money to embolden her to head for Broadway and test the waters. Just before she left, she had second thoughts. Barbra Streisand had just made it big. "Oh, hell," she said, "I don't think there is room in show business for two ugly Jewish girls." But there was.

Connection with celebrity was not strange in Hawaii. Many years after the death of Marilyn Monroe, I was sitting at a football game with Goro Arakawa, longtime proprietor of one of Hawaii's most famous general stores, alas driven out of business by invading big-box stores from the Mainland.

We were talking of this and that, and the subject of Joe DiMaggio came up for no reason I can recall, and I told Goro that I had covered the story of their honeymoon in Japan.

"My wife went to school with Marilyn Monroe," Goro said.

Goro spotted the look of incredulity on my face. So a couple of days later, a brown manila envelope arrived in my mail. In it was a copy of a photograph of the Emerson, California Junior High School Glee Club of 1940. And smack in the middle of the Glee Club was the smiling face, autographed "Norma Jean," of Norma Jean Baker, who was in time to become Marilyn Monroe.

And in the second row was the young Japanese-American girl who was to become Mrs. Goro Arakawa.

✳✳✳

One of my favorite columnar sparring partners was Mayor Frank Fasi, a tough ex-Marine who stayed on in Hawaii after World War II and occupied City Hall for decades. We both enjoyed our frequent squabbles over everything from the upkeep of public golf courses to the future of public transport.

Our longest-running public disagreement was over the question of a new stadium to replace ramshackle Honolulu Stadium, which features prominently in these pages. Honolulu Stadium was dear to the hearts of the populace, home to high school and college football, baseball, championship fights, midget auto racing, State Fairs, even Elvis Presley, who made one of his first public appearances there, and stayed an hour after signing autographs.

But the revered old place, begun in 1924, and expanded haphazardly over the years, was built entirely of wood, much of which had become feasts for termites. It had clearly outlived its usefulness. It had no parking, no proper concession stands, its rest rooms were a disgrace and most of its 25,000 "seats" were backless wooden benches. The press box was a shambles, with a rusted tin roof. The whole thing rocked whenever the spectators got excited, and a shower of rust drifted down. I once wrote you had to comb your hair with a magnet after a doubleheader. My desk in the press box, first to the right of the door, was easily located because sometime around 1957, in my drinking days, I had managed to spill the entire contents of a whiskey highball on it, leaving a huge, ugly brown stain.

Some ten years on, after assignments had taken me to locate the Right Dalai Lama, incur the wrath of LBJ in Vietnam, even count the missiles after the Cuban Crisis, I found myself back behind the same press box desk staring at the same bourbon-colored blotch. In columns I regularly commented on this fact as proof of the slovenly state of the place and lack of upkeep, in my efforts to convince Mayor Frank it was time to stump up for a new one. That, of course, was the rub. Who would pay for a replacement? Frank said as far as he was concerned if he had to finance a new one out of the City coffers the old place was just fine with him. I leaned on him repeatedly to fund a new place to play and the Mayor finally called a press conference to announce: "It would be cheaper to buy Jim Becker a new press box desk, and that is as far as I am willing to go."

Frank stuck by his financial guns, although he never did buy me a new desk, and eventually the State government paid for 50,000-seat Aloha Stadium, a size they hoped would lure a National Football League team. They may have wished they hadn't. No NFL team arrived. The place turned out to be too big for baseball and Hawaii's minor league team gave up and left town. It spoiled the homey atmosphere of high school football and even the students stopped attending games. Many "rust-proof" beams rusted, and the cost of maintenance and repairs long ago exceeded the original price.

Mayor Frank was probably right all along, as he repeatedly reminded me.

✳✳✳

One day in the office of the newspaper's editor, I made an interesting discovery. The editor had just bought a new globe, one of those that stand waist-high and are about a yard in diameter, and he and I were inspecting it, making idle chatter.

"I grew up in Pennsylvania," the editor said, "and I always believed that if you dug a hole straight through the earth from Pennsylvania you would come out in China."

"I grew up in California," I said, "and we believed the same thing. One of us must be wrong."

We decided to check it out. The editor put his finger on his home state, and I crawled around under the globe to find the exact opposite spot. Indian Ocean. Long way from China. We tried California. Same result. Curious, we checked all 49 states, including Alaska. Any one digging a hole through the earth from any of them would get wet at the other end.

"Try Hawaii," the editor said. And we discovered that Hawaii is the only one of the 50 states to have an inhabited antipode. (Pronounced, against all indications, "an-tee-podh," not "an-tup-oh-dee," as it should in any sensible scheme of pronunciation.) Hawaii's antipode is a place called Botswana, and it couldn't be more different. Landlocked, as opposed to Hawaii where one is rarely out of sight of the sea, desert-like (it rains about once every seven years), brown rather than green.

"Go down there and check it out," the editor ordered, so Betty and I took off to travel exactly halfway around the world. We planned to stop in South Africa, which borders Botswana, for a few days to write about the apartheid scene then prevalent there. The authorities had other ideas. Newspapermen were not welcome, particularly those from places where the population is overwhelmingly non-white, and we were ordered to take the next plane out of town. I was magnanimous about it. "I've been thrown out of lots of better places than this," I smiled.

We did stay in Johannesburg long enough to discover there were eight separate toilets at the airport. White, Bantus, Coloured and Asian, men and women. Bantus meant blacks, Coloured meant mixed, Asians meant Indians and Pakistanis, not Japanese or Chinese who probably had to fend for themselves. When I told our Filipina goddaughter—who is Spanish-Visayan-American-Ilocano with a dash of Chinese—about it, she asked, "Where would I go?" "In the bushes, honey," I had to reply.

We also visited the city's finest park. It was full of benches marked "Whites Only," which reminded me of my wartime service in the American South. In the park playground was a sign: "For White Children Only." And in the center, the holy of holies, the most bigoted sign I have ever seen: "For White Children in the Arms of Their Mothers Only." No Bantu nursemaids here.

Botswana was a totally different story. The terrain might be foreign but the people were the same welcoming, friendly ones we had left in Botswana's antipode, Hawaii. We went on safari (cameras, no guns), watched lion prides, were charged by hippos (most unfriendly beasts), awed by elephants, charmed by giraffes. We visited schools. We asked about the university. There was none. Furthermore, the entire country boasted just 23 university graduates, including the Prime Minister and tribal chief, who had been middleweight boxing champion at Oxford.

Betty and I decided something had to be done about that. We wanted to take home to Hawaii a boy and a girl and put them through the University of Hawaii. The Prime Minister thought it was a good idea, but could not provide us with a girl with the necessary qualifications. The only girl we found who had the equivalent of a high school diploma explained to Betty that she had to cheat to get it. Education was for boys, and classes were regularly held under the trees, and she told Betty she used to sneak into the tree and eavesdrop, and with the knowledge thus acquired she got her high school credentials. We couldn't have her, however, because she had an important post in the government.

We settled for two boys. The government of Botswana paid their airfare to Hawaii, the University gave them four-year scholarships and two Hawaii families took them in. Readers sent me money so they could have some walk-around cash for clothes and things. And they both did fine and got their degrees, and went home and did good work there.

The host families have been to Botswana as their guests, and I regularly receive African garments and carved objects from our two University of Hawaii alums.

Betty and I thought that was the end of a good story until we recently received an invitation to help celebrate Botswana Independence Day in Honolulu. We went along to a meeting room at Hawaii Pacific University, another of the colleges in Hawaii, which we found half-filled with smiling, friendly faces, exuding an air of health and happiness. And there we were informed that at that moment, there were in various Hawaii universities no fewer than 38 students from Botswana—and 25 of them were girls.

And with that announcement, all 25 leaped to their feet and high-fived each other.

23.
REVISITING PEARL HARBOR

Vacationing in Honolulu, I was drafted to write the tenth anniversary story of the bombing of Pearl Harbor on December 7, 1941. For the story I interviewed a girl who with her sisters was happily planning her 13th birthday party when the planes came. She still had the skirt with a bullet hole in the hem from a Japanese plane which strafed her front yard which was close to the edge of Pearl Harbor. Scared, shaken but unharmed, she decided it was no day for a party.

The story also featured one of several sailors from the battleship Oklahoma, which capsized during the attack, and one of the men who rescued him, 24 hours later, when they heard tapping on the bottom of the ship. The trapped men had climbed up to the ship bottom and found pockets of air.

The 15th anniversary story—I was Chief of the AP Bureau in 1956— told of how dozens of Honolulu doctors had gathered for a Sunday breakfast to hear a talk from a visiting surgeon on the treatments of wounds. The doctor began with a quote from the Scriptures: "Be ye also ready, for in the hour that ye know not, the Son of Man cometh..."

And the Japanese planes struck. Many of the doctors were to treat real wounds shortly.

And for the *Star-Bulletin* I wrote the 25th anniversary story about Capt. Mitsuo Fuchida and the American intelligence officers on the ground. I won writing prizes for it.

I later learned that Capt. Fuchida, fighter pilot turned Christian evangelist, had teamed up with an American wartime flier, one of the so-called Doolittle Raiders who bombed Tokyo in April 1942 in retaliation for Pearl Harbor. Fuchida had been scheduled to lead the Japanese attack on Midway Island, west of Hawaii, in June 1942, but was in a hospital ship sick bay with appendicitis. The Japanese lost all four carriers and most of their pilots in the Battle of Midway, one of the turning points of the war. Later, Fuchida was on an official military inspection tour in Hiroshima when the first atomic bomb was dropped on August 6, 1945, and again escaped unharmed. Beginning to think his life was spared for a purpose, he turned to Christianity and began touring the United States preaching the gospel.

The Doolittle raid, led by Gen. James Doolittle, consisted of 16 bombers with five-man crews which took off from the deck of an aircraft carrier some 500 miles from the Japanese mainland. After they dropped their bombs—which did little damage but were an immense morale boost to America—they flew to China, and bailed out when their fuel was exhausted. Sixty-nine of the 80 fliers were rescued and taken to safety by Chinese civilians, three died in the parachute drops and eight were captured by the Japanese. They executed four of the fliers and put the other four in prison near Shanghai. One of the prisoners was given a Bible to read, and he was inspired to be a Christian evangelist. On his travels he met Capt. Fuchida, who was on the same mission, and they frequently appeared together at revival meetings.

When Fuchida died in 1973, the Doolittle Raider presided at his funeral services.

On the 25th anniversary of the attack, Capt. Fuchida met with the two American intelligence officers on the ground that day in a house overlooking Pearl Harbor. I was invited to listen in, along with a few Honolulu residents who witnessed the raid.

Gen. Kendell Fielder, the intelligence chief, recalled that he and General Short, the Army commander, were driving home from a party the night of December 6, 1941, and looked down at Pearl Harbor, lights blazing away. General Short remarked, "What a target that would make," Fielder recalled. "Neither of us dreamed it would be one in a few hours."

Capt. Fuchida said the target was also a complete surprise to the pilots until just days before the attack. He said he was the only one the planning chiefs had let in on the secret.

Fuchida said training for the mission had begun three months before. When the pilots saw that they were preparing to attack a harbor with a narrow entrance and shallow water, Fuchida said they immediately thought "Singapore."

Then when the fleet assembled in the far north, they surmised they were going to hit Vladivostok.

"Nobody thought Pearl Harbor," Fuchida recalled. "When we were at sea I called the pilots together and when I told them the target they clapped their hands in surprise."

Gen. Fielder said the fleet was neatly at anchor that day because the commanders were under orders to bring their men in on the weekends for rest. In fact, one commander who failed to do so had been relieved a few weeks earlier.

The weekend rest periods were considered necessary because the fleet spent weekdays in intensive training and regular practice alerts, said Col. George Bicknell, Fielder's deputy.

I remember thinking at the time of Winston Churchill's World War II remark that we take our weekends in the country and our foes take their countries on the weekend.

Nevertheless, Fuchida had been impressed with the quick American reaction. He said his pilots were receiving return fire within five minutes. "I thought 'very good,'" Fuchida recalled. "I think it would have taken the Japanese navy maybe an hour."

I remember someone in the group asked Fuchida if the attackers thought Japan could win the war they were starting that day. He said they didn't concern themselves with that, merely concentrating on their mission.

Fuchida recalled he had confidence his planes could cripple the American fleet at anchor, although he did not expect to return from the mission.

"When we passed over the coastline of Oahu and saw everything was calm and peaceful, I knew we would succeed," he said.

Fielder said he was starting preparations for his daughter's wedding scheduled for the following Friday, bridesmaids and all, when he heard a great explosion. He remembered that his first thought was of sabotage, the prevailing fear among the military chiefs.

Then he looked out and saw smoke coming from Pearl Harbor, and the attacking planes.

Fielder got a call through to Washington and told them Pearl Harbor was under attack. "They were amazed," he said. "Call us back, call us back with the details," he remembered the authorities in the capital told him.

Fielder rushed to headquarters and didn't get home for four days. (His daughter's wedding was postponed. She got married three weeks later. No bridesmaids.)

By now I noticed the lights of Pearl Harbor were twinkling below, as they had the night of December 6, 1941.

As Fuchida prepared to leave, he told us his oldest son was an architect in New York and was working on what would be the world's tallest buildings, taller than the Empire State building. We thought little of it at the time, but Fuchida's son was part of the team designing the World Trade Center towers that would be the target of the 9/11 attack.

After the pilot-turning Christian evangelist left, the two intelligence officers mused, "He seems like a sincere fellow."

I remember Bicknell adding, "He was just doing a job."

Fielder said, "You do try to forgive and forget." Then he paused, "I lost a lot of friends that day."

24.
THE DAY OF THE GOVERNORS

Amid wars and riots, crises and controversies, out of my writing machine came a simple story about ordinary people, a bunch of high school kids from the kind of neighborhood I grew up in; kids whose names would never appear in the paper unless they stabbed the math teacher; kids who seemed doomed to have to try to fight their way out with one hand figuratively tied behind their backs.

These kids were members of the football team of Farrington High School in the least salubrious section of Honolulu. The school teams are nicknamed the Governors, because the school is named after Hawaii's sixth territorial governor from 1921 to 1929. Governor Wallace Rider Farrington, who championed proper public schooling for the children of sugar and pineapple plantation workers who had been imported from China and Japan and the Philippines and Puerto Rico and some of the Pacific islands. This was in the face of opposition from the plantation owners—the Big Five—who once editorially insisted in their own newspaper: "Don't educate them past their station." (I am pleased to note that in recent years, the Farrington High School newspaper, *The Governor*, has been named Overall Best school newspaper several times in the annual Hawaii State High School Journalism Awards competition.)

In 1965, the team from Farrington was scheduled to play the championship game in the traditional Thanksgiving double-header at the venerable old wooden, termite-wrecked Honolulu Stadium, now demolished. The stadium was host to many greats of athletics and entertainment. Joe DiMaggio and Johnny Mize and a host of Hall of Famers played baseball there while in uniform during World War II. Joe Louis fought an exhibition match there, and Jackie Robinson played professional football fresh out of college. Elvis Presley made one of his first public appearances, testing his act in the stadium, and O.J. Simpson sloshed through half an inch of standing water to a touchdown. The high-living pitcher Bo Belinsky hurled a no-hitter for the minor league team and the next day couldn't remember a thing about it.

The Turkey Day double-header, as it was invariably known, was the centerpiece of Honolulu's social and sporting calendar, and 25,000 Honolulu fans, the absolute limit, packed themselves into what they fondly called "The Termite Palace" every year. High school was, and still is, very important to the people of Hawaii, probably because their forebears had to fight so hard to get into, and out of, one. Ask anyone who grew up in Hawaii where they went to school, and they will instantly tell you which *high* school, even though a hefty percentage of them have college degrees.

The Farrington Govs were distinct underdogs in the championship game. Their opponents were from one of Honolulu's big private schools (Kamehameha), which won the championship almost every year. Football is serious business at these academies; players are recruited at an early age from all over the Islands. At Farrington they had to make a team out of the kids who happened to enroll there.

I sensed a subject for a feature story in this David and Goliath pairing involving kids from the neighborhood called Kalihi, where Honolulu's public housing is concentrated; kids from what would be the wrong side of the tracks if Honolulu had any tracks. I telephoned the coach of the Farrington team, and he invited me over to the school.

As would any kid from Foshay, I felt right at home at Farrington. The coach, a big, burly man named Tom Kiyosaki, steely tough, was wearing shorts, as do all football coaches almost all the time, and I could see on his legs the scars where he was wounded in battle with the much-decorated 442nd Regiment, the "Go For Broke" combat team, all volunteers, all Americans of Japanese ancestry from Hawaii and the Mainland.

Kiyosaki, who played his high school football at Maui High, and college ball at the University of Hawaii, had been wounded twice, I later discovered. He recovered from the first wound and rejected an offer to go home and sell War Bonds; instead he rejoined his unit and was wounded again. In his quiet, understated way, Kiyosaki exuded a reminder that we have rights galore, and we also have duties, duties to our country and our community and our family and ourselves. He was a very impressive man.

The Coach told me he was taking his entire team to a hotel in Waikiki to spend the night before the game. He wanted to get his kids out of the housing, where the usual temptations abounded, and away from the gamblers, who prey on high school kids, especially those who have less money in their pockets.

Tom said he had no idea how he was going to pay the hotel bill, but he wanted to give his kids a fair chance to play the most important game of their lives.

So we climbed into a wheezy old school bus—Farrington was obviously very low on the priority list for transportation—and drove to Waikiki, where the kids were housed three to a room and the rest of us drew small singles.

And after we were all settled, the kids walked down to the fancy part of the beach at Waikiki. I noticed they seemed to walk carefully, and talk quietly, and when they reached the sandy strip they looked it over as if it was a foreign country, and I realized that they had been born and bred no more than three miles away, but it had never occurred to them to invade the high-toned hotel country.

The next day, after the kids rubbed the sleep out of their eyes, Tom took the team to a restaurant in Waikiki for their pre-game meal. He had no idea who was going to pay for that, either.

And when the kids finished eating, they all got up and took their dirty dishes out to the kitchen of the restaurant. Tom had trained them that way. Every day, Tom and the other coaches bummed day-old packages of breakfast food, and buns and muffins, fruit and milk, and sat his kids down to the breakfast too many of them never got at home. And when they finished eating, they all took their dirty dishes to the kitchen of the school cafeteria.

Soon it was time to put on their football uniforms and then clamber onto the bus—I couldn't believe fifty kids could be so quiet—and make the short ride to the Termite Palace where 25,000 people were waiting. Some of the spectators didn't even know what team they were.

The players walked into the dressing room reserved for the team and gathered around their captain, John Kameenui, who reminded his teammates of the unprecedented opportunity the Govs were experiencing.

He led the team in a heartfelt prayer and a few of the players wept. I knew I was in the midst of some special people.

And then they went out and won the game—the last public high school to win the City Championship in the old Termite Palace—and the band played the Farrington Alma Mater. John Kameenui and Lippy cried, and so did Speedy Gonzales and Amby Costa.

Amby, who had played the entire game and had a bloody cut on his nose, was joined by his proud girlfriend who escorted him to the bus. "I'll see you later," he told her, "I've got to ride back to school with the team."

And I went to the newspaper office, and I wrote all night. I wrote the longest story in the history of Hawaii journalism.

I told the story of the last day together of the champions, and the newspaper put it on the front page—a story about a bunch of high school kids from Kalihi, on the front page—under a big black headline: "The day the Govs won it all…"

And the story reverberated through Kalihi, and then all of Hawaii—and it hasn't stopped yet.

The headline became part of the language. An entire chapter of the book that tells the history of newspapers in Hawaii is devoted to the Farrington story.

People in Kalihi realized that maybe they were worth something after all.

More than half the kids on the football team went on to college, something previously unheard of.

Since, we have had a two-term Governor of the State from Farrington. And a Chief of Police. Emme Tomimbang, our leading television personality was a cheerleader on the championship team.

Incidentally, two anonymous people came forward and paid the hotel bill and the restaurant tab, respectively.

And not so long ago, we were having dinner at a fancy restaurant in Waikiki, and when I asked for the check, the manager came to our table and said:

"No check, Mr. Becker. I went to Farrington. You made us proud."

And of all the things I've written, I'm proudest of that.

THE DAY THE GOVS WON IT ALL
Honolulu Star-Bulletin
Friday, November 26, 1965

The team bus is a wheezing rusty hulk of a 1942 model, driven by a garbage collector on his day off.

The trainer is a merchant seaman named Flash who misses all the ships during the football season.

The coach spends much of his time scrounging surplus milk and cut-rate breakfast food so some of his boys who don't eat properly at home can get some nourishment.

The neighborhood is so tough that a couple of years ago thieves stripped bare every car in the faculty parking lot—except the football coach's car.

Out of this material came the 1965 champions of the violent world of prep football, the Farrington Governors. This is the story of their last day together.

Ambrose Costa sat on the edge of the crumpled bed in a Waikiki hotel room and picked up his wine-red football helmet with the white top hat painted on the sides and the large number "29" on the back.

"Gee, today is gonna be my last day wearing this thing," he said.

"It's been with me so long. It's just like losing a part of me."

He put the helmet down on the floor, and picked up his jersey and began to pull it over his head.

A fellow wearing number 62 rushed through the open door of the room, and plunked himself down hard on the bed against the wall.

"Oh," said Charles Lacaden, the stocky guard. "I got butterflies."

"You got butterflies?" said Costa. "I don't."

"I guess this game is too big," said Lacaden.

Leslie Kent, the fullback, who wears 30 on his shirt, popped in, football shoes in his hand. "Iolani's ahead, 6-0," he said.

"You better fix your spike," said Costa, pointing to one of the cleats on Kent's shoes that had worked loose from its moorings.

"Yeah," said Kent, absently. "Man, we better win today."

"Don't tell me," said Costa. "You're looking at a member of the 1965 champions."

"Yeah, man," said Kent. "I want that medal."

"I want Kalihi to be the best," said Lacaden.

"You got that blocking straight?" Costa asked Kent. "The side I pinch is the way you go."

"If you pinch me on the right side, I go right?" asked Kent. "Maybe they'll see it. How about a code word?"

"Okay," said Costa. "How do you say 'right' in Samoan?"

Kent said something that sounded like: "Toomatoo."

"And left?"

This sounded like "to-ooavalei."

"Forget it," said Costa. "Look. I'll say 'R.' That means 'right.' Okay?"

"Five minutes," said a voice in the hall outside. "Five minutes more."

The three players stood up and all the smiles were gone, and they shook hands solemnly, calling each other by their last names. "Good luck, Costa," "Good luck, Lacaden." And they began picking up their equipment to head for the bus.

Outside, in the long lobby of the Coco Palms Hotel, other football players were walking slowly, quietly, toward the door. It was 1:40 p.m.

Kickoff for the 1965 Honolulu Inter-scholastic League championship game was an hour and 20 minutes away, and the time for laughing was over. The hotel—which had rocked with the horse-play and high spirits of 50-odd high school football players—had begun to quiet down about an hour before.

Now it was butterfly time, the time when the mouth gets dry and the jokes get old and fellows who are going to have to carry the load—the half dozen players who are the backbone of the team—began making the first of six or seven trips they will make to the bathroom before game time.

The Farrington team had arrived at the Coco Palms Hotel just before dark, on Wednesday afternoon.

"I wanted to get them all together, and keep them together," said Tom Kiyosaki, the blunt, unemotional man who came to Farrington as head football coach seven years ago.

"Two years ago we played Kam for the title, and friends took the kids out for dinner before the game and kept them up late. And a lot of the kids, maybe eight out of ten, come from the housing area. And they get a lot of crank calls, and stuff.

207

"I get 'em, too, and letters calling me a juicer, and all that, and I expect it. But how can people do that to kids? How can they stoop so low?"

Kiyosaki crossed his bare legs—it was early morning and the coach was sitting in the hotel lobby in sweat shirt and shorts and leather slippers—and you could see the spot where shrapnel ripped through his right leg during the war.

(He picked up two Purple Hearts with the 442nd, one in Italy and one in France, but he went on to play four years of football at the University of Hawaii, and then got into coaching.)

"So I told my principal we had to get the boys together, down here. We got a very good rate, two-sixty a night, with three boys to a room, and we'll find the money someplace.

"We took 18 rooms, and the hotel threw in two rooms for the coaches, free. We have five coaches, including me, but one couldn't come last night.

"This way we will have control of the food the boys eat before the game, too.

"You know, I'm the councilor at Farrington, so I work with these boys all year, and they have so many problems.

"I found out some of them don't eat breakfast or lunch. So I fixed it with the cafeteria so they save me all the milk they have left over, and we buy big cartons of cereals—the cafeteria buys it for me, they get a rate—and we feed 'em, so they'll have something.

"Football has done wonders for these kids. They learn to like orders, and they learn respect. They say 'Yes, sir.'"

A couple of seconds later, the doorway was half-filled by Ambrose Costa, who is only five-nine and 170 pounds, but seems much larger.

Ambrose was wearing a neat white shirt and grey slacks. His feet were bare, and his kinky hair was tousled.

He has frank, brown eyes, very clear and very honest looking, and fine, white teeth when he smiles. His nose comes down almost straight from his forehead, and it was running.

"Amby's had a cold," Kiyosaki explained.

"Don't take any cold pills today," he said to Costa. "They might make you dizzy."

Then the coach went off to look after the rest of the boys, and Costa sat down on the lobby couch.

He is the center on offense and the middle linebacker on defense and he plays every minute of every game as long as the issue is in doubt. He talks a lot when he gets started and he talks well.

That seems to be the mark of a Kiyosaki player. The coach does not talk Pidgin to the players and they do not talk Pidgin to him, nor to each other, much of the time.

(And in all the time I spent with the team on their day, I never once heard any of the cruder four letter words.)

"Boy, if we'd played 'em last night, we'd have beat 'em," Costa said.

"We had a meeting, all of us in one room, and we brought everything out. We held nothing back.

"We figured we got to be one group today. Tears came down.

"You know, all year, we practice in full pads, and we scrimmage. We never get to work out in shorts, and just run dummy drills, like some teams do, sometimes, and sometimes we feel like we'd like to take it easy.

"But you know, it was good for us. And the coaches took us to Las Vegas for a game, and Disneyland, and now this hotel. We've got to pay them back.

"We said that, and we said, if we really love our fathers, the least we can do is really work, and make them proud of us. So they can say they have a son who played for a championship team.

"Then he can really hold up his head."

A couple of other players walked through the lobby, and Costa pointed them out.

"That's Walt Rodrigues," he said. "The end. We call him 'Lippy,' because he's always talking. He can make a rhyme out of anything, in a second.

"And that's Tommy. Tommy Gushiken. We call him 'Speedy Gonzales.' He can really run. I was telling him the other day in a couple of years he'll be the world's fastest human.

"And there's Joe Gomes. We call him 'Snow.' He's kinda dark, but we named him after Jack Snow, the end for Notre Dame. Joe's got real sticky fingers.

"We call Frank Gaspar, the tackle, 'Filongi.' That's Samoan for Frank. And James Kalili, the other tackle, is 'Bear.' Because he looks like one, and he's about as tough as one.

"And Stan Cadiente, the quarterback, he's 'Stan the Man.' And Allan Yap is 'Dizzy.' He's always getting mixed up.

"We've got a name for everybody. This is one year when we had a team. Nobody fought against each other, and when we made a mistake, nobody yelled at the guy but we all tried to cheer him up.

"Last year, we had a lot of grumbling in the huddle and like that, but not this year. You feel good playing with a bunch of guys like this.

"Like yesterday. We all wore shirts and ties to school so everybody would know us, and know we were a team.

"Then we came over here to the hotel, and we had a box lunch, lau lau and rice and long rice and we went to the movie. It was 'King Rat.' We liked it, and a lot of the guys gathered around the organ, down front. Gosh, it's got so many keys and buttons.

"I wish I was musical. All I can do is sing.

"After the movie we had the meeting, and then some of the guys played 'Trumps.' Do you know how to play it? It's a card game, where you deal out all the cards, and then one side names the trumps—you bid for it—and if, say, diamonds are led and you don't have any, you play a trump and you take that pack.

"And then we went to sleep. I slept pretty good, but Tommy didn't.

"He and I and Pat Oka went down to the water this morning, and we were looking at the little fish, and Tommy said he was thinking all night, about the game. He said he could see the kickoff coming all night.

"And Pat said, 'Yeah, Tommy was moaning all night.'

"But I slept good."

It was getting close to 10:30 now, and "Nappy" Napoleon, who ordinarily drives a garbage truck for the city but who drives the ancient Farrington bus as a volunteer, had arrived.

Coach Kiyosaki called the team together, in the parking lot behind the hotel.

"We're going to the Harvest Moon in Waikiki," he said. "For our meal. You know this was a last minute deal, and we couldn't get what we wanted, because most of the places are booked up for the holiday.

"We tried to get you steaks, but we may have to settle for hamburger.

"Now, not too much gravy. And after you eat, wait in the bus and we will come back as a team. Don't go wandering around Waikiki.

"When we get back, you can rest. We start taping at 1:30, and the bus will leave at 1:45 sharp.

"That clear?"

"Yes, sir," snapped the players.

"Okay, let's go."

And at the Harvest Moon, the most surprised girl in Honolulu was Jeannie Nohara, a bubbly girl who appeared to be in charge, and who had never heard of the arrangements that had been made to feed about 50 hungry football players on Thanksgiving morning.

"But we can do it," she said. "I'm a Farrington grad myself."

In the kitchen, the two cooks threw all the hamburger steaks and tenderloin cutlets in the place on the stove. A fellow began opening two huge cans labeled: "Three Sisters Cut Wax Beans. 6 lbs., 5 ozs."

Jeannie began spooning fruit cocktail into small dishes, and a fellow threw a huge pan of rice on the stove.

"Can they eat fried rice?" he asked. "If it's not too greasy," said the coach.

And, somehow, the food was prepared, and the fellows went out to the kitchen to get it, cafeteria-style, and then they brought their empty dishes back.

Coach Kiyosaki sat at the end of the room, toying with his food, and finally he got up and gave a couple of his cutlets to the players.

In a few minutes, the players were back in the bus and on their way back to the hotel. Nappy pulled the bus up to the front.

"This is a first class team," he said, "and we use the front door."

The wives of two of the assistant coaches, Moana Espinda and Mahealani Fellez, were waiting.

"We came to get our good luck kiss," Moana said, and they did.

"Now we've got to get to the game or we won't find a place to park. Our husbands can go in the bus." Moana pointed to the battered old thing.

"Isn't it pitiful?" she said. "It's a 1942, although I don't suppose there's anything original left on it. One time last year it caught fire, on the way to a basketball game, and they had to stop and borrow hoses from the people in the neighborhood."

Coach Kiyosaki said that Farrington has acquired a new bus from military surplus, and that it will be ready for "Nappy" in a month or two.

"'Nappy is one of three volunteer drivers we have," Kiyosaki said. "They are all brothers, and they all drive garbage trucks for the city.

"Flash Silva, our trainer, is a volunteer, too. He just misses all the ships during the football season.

"There are a lot of people out our way who help out. Football means a lot to the people in Kalihi.

"You know, it's a very rough neighborhood, and a lot of things go on there. One time, it was three years ago, we were playing a game and some cars were parked in the campus lot, and they stripped every one of them, right down to the tires, except mine.

"The police called me in and wanted to know how come they left mine alone."

And now Kiyosaki and the players drifted off to their rooms to rest. And then it was time for Flash and the coaches to tape up the players, and then time to pick up the helmets and pads and shake hands and get in the bus.

The Day of the Governors

On the way to the Stadium, Cadiente, the brilliant quarterback, sat and looked steadily, quietly, out the window.

Lippy Rodrigues had nothing to say, until the bus pulled up behind the Diamond Head stands.

"Gee, even the cheap seats are full," he said.

A kid selling newspapers on the street shouted out: "What team is that?"

"Haven't you heard of the Farrington Governors?" said Lippy.

The team trampled into the locker room, cleats rattling on the cement floor. Cadiente, Costa, big John Kameanui—the three captains—and a couple of others sprawled out flat on the floor, their feet stuck up on benches.

"Five minutes," said a man who stuck his head in the door, and the coach called the team together.

Kameenui spoke up first.

"This is it," he said. "Our last game for the school. Maybe it will be a long time before Farrington has this opportunity again.

"Now close your eyes and get down on your knees."

Kameenui knelt in the middle, and said, "We pray for guidance, we pray that no one gets injured, on their team or our team. And we pray that all play our best game. For our school and our families and our teammates."

When they got up, at least six or seven of the players were weeping. Coach Kiyosaki stepped up.

"Now relax," he said. "We've all got butterflies. It's only natural. I want you to know that we're very proud of all of you, win or lose.

"And this is the game. This is the one we wanted. We worked for this. We prayed for this.

"Now clear your minds, and play as hard as you can."

The team started for the door, but big John Kameanui stopped them. "Hold it." he said. "We dedicate this game to the coaches.

"Now give me three 'alu's.' One-two-three . . . alu. One-two-three . . . alu. One-two-three . . . alu."

The call—it means "go" in Hawaiian—was grunted out, sharp and loud, each time.

And then it was time to play. Kamehameha got off in front, 6-0, but the Farrington Governors fought back with a pass from Stan the Man to Lippy, and then Stan the Man battled over for two points, and the score was 8-6 at halftime.

In the dressing room, Coach Kiyosaki drew some diagrams on the board, and arranged some new defenses.

"Now let's not ease up because we're ahead," he said. "We've got 24 more minutes to play before we take them."

"Yes, sir," snapped the players. And then, with less than four minutes to play, Stan the Man arched a perfect pass to Speedy Gonzales and a couple of minutes later he hit Lippy again for a touchdown, and the two-point conversion was good.

Now it was 16-6, and Farrington couldn't lose, but Kiyosaki stood on the sidelines and stared at the play until the gun actually went off.

His coaches threw their arms around him, and he looked away and bit hard on his lip, but he couldn't stop the tears. He gulped, over and over, and then he got hold of himself and wiped his eyes.

Somebody stuck the football in his hand, and people kept coming up and shaking his hand, so finally he had to hand the football to young Ken, who took it and stared at it up close with big round eyes.

"Thank you, thank you," Kiyosaki said, over and over, but he looked at the ground and tried not to weep again.

And then the band played the Farrington Alma Mater song, a corny sort of thing that might be the song of any high school in the land, and John Kameenui cried so hard that his big body shook, and Lippy cried and so did Speedy Gonzales. The Bear cried and Filongi.

And Amby Costa looked serious, but his eyes were clear. He had played every second of the game; and there was a small cut on his nose, the blood oozing slowly out.

Then the song was over, and suddenly Amby Costa was joined by a pretty girl—her name is Rochelle Mott, and she is his girl—who took his helmet, the one he will never wear again, from his hand and carried it in hers.

They walked along through the crowd, banging into people and not even noticing, until they came to the gate, and then Ambrose took his helmet back.

"I'll see you later," he said. "I've got to ride back to school with the team."

✳✳✳

WHERE ARE THEY NOW?

"My daughter tells me you are her school counselor," said Stan Cadiente, the quarterback, to Tom Gushiken, the speedy running back, now a coach and counselor at Waipahu High School on Leeward Oahu.

"Yes. I told her we were teammates. She seemed surprised," said Gushiken.

"She didn't know I played football," said Cadiente, passer, punter, place kicker, signal caller and undisputed leader of the Farrington High School team that won the City championship on Thanksgiving Day, 1965, the Day the Govs Won it All.

The exchange between the two men, now in their late 50's, pointed up how the lives of the players on that special team that captured the hearts of a community are intertwined even unto the next generation. A tightly-knit group then, the players are mostly still close, easy with each other.

Over the years they have attended each other's weddings, and the occasional funeral, coached each other's kids, played golf and softball together, collected for a reunion whenever one of their teammates now living on the Mainland came home for a visit and gathered semi-regularly just to be together and "talk story," as the local jargon has it. When the Little League team from Ewa Beach, about a dozen miles

215

from Kalihi, won the 2005 World Series and the adulation of all, many minds turned back to the Farrington team that had won all hearts 40 years before.

And how have the Farringtonians fared over the four decades? The *Honolulu Advertiser* newspaper organized a gathering of teammates in order to take stock, and invited me along.

Tom Gushiken remembered: "When Ewa Beach won the World Series it was just like what happened to us, We were celebrities in our time. It meant so much to the community when we won it all." About a dozen of his teammates, who drifted in and out of a "talk story" session at the house of Gordon Hunter, a lineman on the team, agreed. Hunter's house is a convenient meeting place. He is the only member of the team who still lives in the old Kalihi neighborhood.

"When the families started to come we all moved away," remembered Cadiente. "And some guys went to college on the Mainland and never came back."

Hunter is the unofficial team historian. His records showed that 40 years on, three of the 45 players on the championship roster had died, and contact had been lost with three others. "But we're trying to get in touch with them through their families here in town," Hunter said.

A final count showed that 28 of the 45 went to college, a rarity at the time, and 15—one-third—have four-year degrees or better. About two-thirds of the players still live and work in Hawaii. All appear comfortable, some are thriving, a few quite definitely so.

"We have a ton of schoolteachers," Hunter said. "And a lawyer, a deputy sheriff, a couple of cops, an airline pilot and Howard Miyashiro is vice president of a bank. "And Walter Rodrigues, who is still known as Lippy, has a highly-paid position on the docks. One of our teammates got into trouble with the law, but he has straightened his arrow out and is working in the tourist industry in Waikiki. In fact, he just brought out his own line of T-shirts. On the Mainland we have two guys who work for airlines, one who sells cars in North Carolina and John Kameenui is area manager for one of the big box stores. We hear he may be coming home to manage some of their stores here."

"That would be a change," said Allan Yap, the 160-pound fullback who is one of the many high school teachers produced by the team. "We sent him a ticket to our 25th reunion and he only got as far as Las Vegas. He called us from there."

"Then there is Jimmy Kalili, the big tackle," said Hunter. "He had a fabulous college playing career and was drafted by the Washington Redskins, but he got homesick and left training camp. He is big in the Hawaiian sovereignty movement on the Big Island, and he sometimes gets into trouble for trespassing, stuff like that, and when he does his teammate, Steve Lim, who is a lawyer, bails him out."

The lives of Cadiente and Gushiken are patterns for the life path followed by many of the players on that team of destiny. Cadiente played junior college football in Arizona, came home to marry his high school girlfriend, had four kids, and is now a supervisor at the *Advertiser* newspaper's suburban printing plant. He still weighs 150 pounds, his playing weight. (His younger brother, also a Farrington quarterback, is a sportswriter for the other newspaper.) Gushiken, who was the fastest man in the league and maybe the whole State, played baseball in college in Kansas, met and married his wife there, and had a career coaching sports in high school and at the University of Hawaii. He has added a good 25 pounds to his game weight.

Among the departed is Tom Kiyosaki, the twice-wounded war veteran coach, with the stern manner and marshmallow heart. Still remembered by the players how he and the other coaches, Eckie Espinda and Harry Pacarro, spent much of their time scrounging milk and fruit and breakfast food to feed those of their players who didn't eat properly at home. The players are in regular touch with Coaches Espinda and Pacarro, and their wives, who in their time fed and housed dozens of Farrington athletes from troubled homes. Nappy Napoleon, the city garbage truck driver, who volunteered to drive the tattered old Farrington bus, and Flash Silva, the merchant seaman who served as the team's unpaid trainer, have both died.

But the players still talk regularly with their most-storied volunteer, Dr. Tommy Chang. When the authorities decreed that high schools had to have a doctor in attendance at all games but neglected to provide any funds for that purpose, Dr. Chang not only walked the Farrington sidelines for decades but treated injured athletes, in season and out, with no thought of any fee.

While taking stock, the players figured that at a rough guess they have at least 70 or 80 children among them, probably more. "Frank Gaspar, the big tackle, leads the parade," said Joe Gomes, a slick pass-catching end in high school who had added at least 75 pounds and calls himself the "last of the beach boys." It was never easy, then and now, for Gomes to get serious. "Last time I saw him he had a slew of grandchildren."

And then, as it always does when old teammates get together, the talk turned to championship days, and Coach Kiyosaki. "Remember Toots Kahanui? Coach Kiyosaki kicked him off the team for always coming to school late. We told him to go back and ask for another chance, and Coach said, 'Okay, but you have to come to school 15 minutes early every day and raise the flag.' And he did. For the whole year."

"Remember those notes on yellow paper that meant Coach wanted to see you in his office? One guy got one and went in, shaking in his shoes, and Coach handed him a slip of paper and said: 'You're going to this college.'"

Then Joe Gomes got semi-serious. "We had one team," he said, emphasizing the last word.

"Nobody talked in the huddle but Stan," said Lippy. "He was the man."

"We had chop suey," said Gomes. "Filipino, Japanese, Chinese, Samoan backfield, Hawaiians and big hapa-haoles, on the line."

"And Portuguese line backers," said Lippy, who was one.

"And the main thing we had was love," said Gomes.

"If we had so much love how come Gordon (Higa) and I didn't get to play more?" asked Hunter.

"We didn't have that much love," said Lippy, as quick with a quip as ever.

More 40-year-old memories flooded out, sometimes two men talking at once, sometimes one starting and another finishing a story.

"Horace Todd was one of the few guys on the team who had a car. And we went to play Kalani (High School), and when we got back on the bus his car was up on cement blocks and somebody had stolen all the wheels. One of our guys knew a man who had a junk yard and we had to go there and get four wheels so he could drive home."

"Remember Socks Woodley? We didn't have much good equipment at Farrington in those days, and the good helmets and pads and football shoes went to Stan and the other starters. The rest of us had to scramble around in a big pile of old shoes and try to find a pair that matched, never mind fit. And Socks put tape all over his shoes and the coaches asked him why, and it turned out he was trying to hide the fact that he had no socks. Couldn't afford to buy white socks. The coaches got him some, and we always called him Socks after that. He became a local softball legend."

"Hard to believe when you look at us now that once some of us couldn't afford to buy socks."

And it is.

EPILOGUE

And so it was, when it was fun.

Retelling these stories stirred memories of talks with Generals Eisenhower, Marshall and MacArthur, often under the wings of airplanes during refueling stops at obscure airfields. I recall arguing with that dessicated calculating machine, Secretary of Defense Robert McNamara, that bombing is useful only if the other side has something worth bombing, and if you hit it. I recall being lectured by the overly active Secretary of State John Foster Dulles who had been advised by Adlai Stevenson, "Don't just do something, stand there." And I remember playing bridge with the economist and former Ambassador to India John Kenneth Galbraith. And I was steered straight on the world picture by the brilliant Soviet expert Chip Bohlen, a regular golfing opponent.

And I recall learning from Nehru of India, Japanese prime ministers, United Nations secretaries-general, Filipino presidents, a king of Malaysia, leaders of Indonesia and Pakistan, a German chancellor, British prime ministers, even Robert Mugabe of Zimbabwe in his saner days, several American presidents, sometimes in a small group, sometimes alone.

These were background discussions, and it turned out that most invariably I was told the truth.

Why? I think because we were adults who would not betray a confidence and who had demonstrated our responsibility to explain complicated issues to readers and viewers. You can't do that until you understand them and that often requires hearing from the movers and shakers. There was mutual trust.

Today that trust has gone, along with the straight talk. Spin is in.

What went wrong? Why have the products of the craft so often turned into a constant monotonous series of like-minded feeding frenzies? Why have priorities switched from telling the story to destroying the characters. How did they lose touch with the concerns of real people?

Newspaper circulation is tumbling. It is axiomatic that no one under 40 buys a newspaper and no one under 30 even reads one. Television newscasts once were watched by more that 90 percent of us. Now, including cable newscasts, it is about half that.

What's to blame?

The prevalence of the Pauline Kael Syndrome is an obvious culprit. She was the superb film critic for the *New Yorker* who, after Nixon had carried 49 states famously said, "How could he win. I don't know anyone who voted for him."

In our palmiest days, we had in the news business everything from card-carrying Communists to charter members of the Flat Earth Society, but it didn't show in their writing. Today it does. The *New York Times* not so long ago killed two columns by staff writers of 30 years' standing because they did not agree with the paper's current obsession. In contrast, during my stint on the *Honolulu Star-Bulletin* I frequently attacked the owner's hotel and real estate development plans in his own newspaper.

The times sure have changed.

Epilogue

Affluence is also to blame. These days, the people who read the tele-prompters and conduct the interviews and pick the contents of the front page are often ensconced in apartments on Fifth Avenue and Central Park West, cheek by jowl with the sort of people you meet in the pages of *People Weekly*. It is difficult to discern the concerns of real people from such havens.

This is not to suggest that we were all shabbily treated in the pay department. The AP was particularly generous, and practically coddled its foreign correspondents. It issued me a pass good on every airline in the world and all major hotels, some years before credit cards were invented, and allowed expense accounts couched in a dozen currencies without demur. Nor were my other employers niggardly in that depart-ment, with me or my colleagues. But none of us collected Monopoly money salaries, and most would have considered inclusion on the social ramble A-list sell-out.

The 24-hour news cycle is perhaps the prime suspect in the changed style of journalism. It is made to order for high-living bottom-feeders. There is little time to reflect or to explain. We are merely swamped with doubtful detail on stories of intense interest only to the editors of other news channels.

Add them up and in our trade we have far too many who want to be the heroes of the story, and far too few willing to serve as witnesses.

The English language takes a beating in the process, even in print. AP recently sent out a story that described something as a "site for sore eyes." Well, it passes the spell checker. And more sadly, I checked on the Internet. At least a dozen newspapers ran the story, and not one corrected it.

Where are the Jack Bergers when we need them?

Perhaps all is not lost forever. Perhaps a sagging readership and dis-appearing viewers will constitute a wake-up call. Perhaps falling prof-its will. Perhaps they may find a way to earn our trust again.

Perhaps they may even learn how to spell. Which is where I came in.

ACKNOWLEDGMENTS

In a long life filled with incident, I have been aided and abetted beyond the call by many, beginning with my parents who steered a house full of kids through the Great Depression with no job and no money and never let us even think of the word "victim," and the Los Angeles Public School System, which opened my ears and eyes.

I owe great gratitude to Jack Berger, the editor who taught me how to do journalism and to Wes Gallagher and Bob Eunson and my other bosses at The Associated Press who turned me loose for so many years on the big stories. To the Army's 27th Wolfhound Regiment and the U.S. Marines, who showed what bravery and comradeship could do in two Asian wars.

To the Philippines, which embraced Betty and me and gave us Tina and Carrie and Ming to cherish. To the people of Hawaii, who made us feel "local" almost on the day of arrival more than 50 years ago and where we are at home today. To the editors of the *Honolulu Star-Bulletin*, who gave me my head and the front page, even when I produced a magazine-length effusion about a bunch of high school kids from the tough side of town.

To Westinghouse and the Voice of America and NBC, which let me learn about microphones and camera angles on the big stages of Europe.

To Londoners Stephen Mead and the Hollings family and friends and Margaret Llamas and our extended Filipino family who enabled and enlivened our cultural wallowing. To Wolfgang and Gudrun Wagner for the Bayreuth experience, like which there is no other. To Jay Buckley whose baseball tours are a real joy and introduced us to the real America and real Americans.

To Jackie Robinson, courage and dignity personified, who carried a nation to higher ground in the wake of his victory over bigotry and hate. To Jack and Barbara Nicklaus, excellence, grace and decency epitomized. To Bud Watkins, the big right-hander who prodded me for years to commit these stories to print, and Sandra Blakeslee who enthusiastically encouraged their publication. And to Bob and Ida Rhea, friends whom success never spoiled and whose great generosity made this publication possible.

To Ed Chun who handled the paper work with great good humor, Sandie Osborne who lovingly edited the copy, to the brilliant illustrator Corky Trinidad, who provided the art work, to Bill Greaves, who designed the book with artistic flair and to Roger Jellinek, literary agent extraordinaire, patient, caring, encouraging, wise and master of the trade, who made the whole thing happen.

And above all, to my wife Betty, who remembers when we were "THE romance of Shanghai" and who civilized me, inspired me, was at my side through many of the adventures detailed here and who saw the book through to the light of day when my eyesight failed.

Bless them all.

ABOUT
THE AUTHOR

Foreign correspondent, sports writer, columnist, music critic, broadcaster, Jim Becker in a long and wide-ranging career might report on a political crisis one month, a major sporting event the next, with a visit to a presentation of Richard Wagner's Ring Cycle in between.

An ace reporter for the *Los Angeles Herald-Express* at the age of 17, after wartime Army service in India and China, he spent a quarter century with the Associated Press, covering wars and international crises as well as major musical and sporting events. He was chief of AP bureaus in pre-Statehood Hawaii, then Manila and New Delhi, where he directed news coverage for all South Asia. He wrote a human interest column for the *Honolulu Star-Bulletin* for nearly a decade, and spent a dozen years in Europe as a broadcaster.

For half a century Jim Becker has been involved in Hawaii's evolution from heavy-handed oligarchy to a society where everyone is in the minority, and racial barriers are down. He is a past president of the Hawaiian Historical Society, was twice Chairman of the Board of

Hawaii Public Television, and served on boards of many major musical organizations in Hawaii. He is a renowned lecturer on opera.

He has been published in numerous anthologies of best news and sports stories, contributed to magazines ranging from *National Geographic* to *Opera News.*